The Complete
IDIOT'S
Guide to
ACCESS

by Paul McFedries

alpha
books

A Division of Prentice Hall Computer Publishing
201 W. 103rd St. Indianapolis, Indiana 46290 USA

International Standard Book Number:1-56761-457-4
Library of Congress Catalog Card Number: 93-74246

96 95 94   8 7 6 5 4 3 2 1

Interpretation of the printing code: the rightmost number of the first series of numbers is the year of the book's printing; the rightmost number of the second series of numbers is the number of the book's printing. For example, a printing code of 94-1 shows that the first printing of the book occurred in 1994.

Screen reproductions in this book were created by means of the program Collage Plus from Inner Media, Inc., Hollis, NH.

Printed in the United States of America

Publisher
Marie Butler-Knight

Acquisitions Editor
Barry Pruett

Managing Editor
Elizabeth Keaffaber

Development Editor
Mary Cole Rack

Production Editor
Michelle Shaw

Copy Editor
San Dee Phillips

Cover Designer
Scott Cook

Designer
Amy Peppler-Adams, Roger Morgan

Illustrations
Steve Vanderbosch

Indexer
Jeanne Clark

Production Team
Gary Adair, Brad Chinn, Kim Cofer, Meshell Dinn, Mark Enochs, Stephanie Gregory, Jenny Kucera, Beth Rago, Marc Shecter, Kris Simmons, Greg Simsic, Carol Stamile, Robert Wolf

Special thanks to C. Herbert Feltner for ensuring the technical accuracy of this book.

Contents at a Glance

This page unintentionally left blank.

Contents

Introduction

When it comes to computers, a "complete idiot" is someone who, despite having the normal complement of gray matter, wouldn't know a hard disk from a hard-boiled egg. This is, of course, perfectly normal and, despite what many so-called computer gurus may tell you, does not imply any sort of character defect on your part.

So, we may as well get one thing straight right off the bat: the fact that you're reading *The Complete Idiot's Guide to Access* does *not* make you an idiot. Quite the opposite, in fact:

- ☛ It shows you have discriminating taste and will settle for nothing less than the best (and it shows that you don't mind immodest authors).

- ☛ It shows you have a gift for self-deprecation (which is just a high-falutin' way of saying that you don't take yourself—or any of this computer business—too seriously).

- ☛ It shows that you're determined to learn this Access thing, but you don't want to bother with a lot of boring, technical details.

- ☛ It shows that you know it doesn't make sense to learn absolutely *everything* about Access. You just need to know enough to get your work done.

- ☛ It shows you know enough not to spend your days reading five bazillion pages of arcane (and mostly useless) information. You do, after all, have a life to lead.

A Book for Smart Access Idiots

This is a book for those of us who aren't (and don't even want to be) computer wizards. This is a book for those of us who have a job to do—a job that includes working with Access—and we just want to get it done as quickly and painlessly as possible. This is *not* one of those absurdly serious, put-a-crease-in-your-brow-and-we'll-begin kinds of books. On the contrary, we'll even try to have—gasp!—a little fun as we go along.

You'll also be happy to know that this book doesn't assume you have any previous experience with Access (or even with Windows, for that matter). This means that we'll begin each topic at the beginning and build your knowledge from there. However, with *The Complete Idiot's Guide to Access*, you get just the facts you *need* to know, not everything there *is* to know. All the information is presented in short, easy-to-digest chunks that you can easily skim through to find just the information you want.

How This Book Is Set Up

I'm assuming you have a life away from your computer screen, so *The Complete Idiot's Guide to Access* is set up so you don't have to read it from cover to cover. If you want to know how to enter data, for example, just turn to the chapter that covers entering and editing data. To make things easier to find, I've organized the book into six more or less sensible sections:

Part I   Feel the Fear and Do It Anyway: Getting Started with Access

The book begins with six chapters designed to get your Access education off on a firm footing. These chapters cover a few crucial Access tasks, give a brief introduction to database concepts, show you how to get Access up and running, and cover important background material on the program's menus, toolbars, and dialog boxes. No sweat. For the finale you'll create your very first Access database.

Part II   Table Manners: Working with Access Tables

Most of your Access work will involve *tables*: the objects that will contain all your data. The seven chapters in Part II introduce you to these ubiquitous creatures and show you how to design them, create them, enter data into them, and customize them to suit your lifestyle. You'll also learn about the oh-so-handy *forms* that can help take the drudgery out of data entry.

Part III   Basic Tools for Taming the Access Beast

Part III covers a few tools that will help you get the most out of Access. You'll learn how to quickly find the data you need from even the most humongous database, how to sort your data to make things more comprehensible, how to use filters to separate the wheat from the chaff, and how to manage those interminable windows that Access will be throwing at you.

Part IV   Ask and Ye Shall Receive: Querying Access Tables

Queries let you, literally, ask questions of your data. They're an essential tool of modern database management, and the three chapters in Part IV tell you everything you need to know.

Part V   Impressing Friends and Family with Access Reports

Once you've entered your data and completed all your sorting, filtering, and querying chores, you'll often need to summarize the whole kit and caboodle into a nice, neat report. Part V shows you how to use Access' reporting features to create reports that are sure to make you a legend around the office.

Part VI   Access Excess: Advanced Topics for the Brave (or Foolhardy)

Access is a powerful program that is just chock full of obscure and technical features that appeal only to tall-forehead types. However, there are a few goodies that can help the rest of us become more productive. Part VI looks briefly at three of these features: customizing the Access program options; using graphics and OLE (Object Linking and Embedding); and working with multiple tables.

The Complete Idiot's Guide to Access also includes the following can't-find-'em-anywhere-else features:

- ☞ An unserious Speak Like a Geek glossary designed to knock some sense into all those bizarre terms that computer geeks like to bandy about.

- ☞ An "Ideas" chapter full of all kinds of interesting, but very practical, suggestions for using Access around the home and office.

- ☞ A handy tear-out reference card that gives you easy access to important Access facts.

Things to Look for in Your Travels

The Complete Idiot's Guide to Access is designed so you can get the information you need fast and then get on with your life. When you need to type something, it will appear in bold, like this:

type this

Look for the following icons that will help you learn just what you need to know:

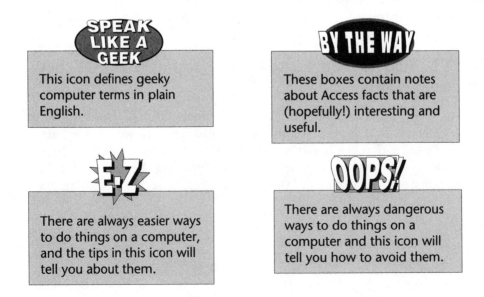

SPEAK LIKE A GEEK

This icon defines geeky computer terms in plain English.

BY THE WAY

These boxes contain notes about Access facts that are (hopefully!) interesting and useful.

E-Z

There are always easier ways to do things on a computer, and the tips in this icon will tell you about them.

OOPS!

There are always dangerous ways to do things on a computer and this icon will tell you how to avoid them.

These tips are for you lucky folks with Version 2.0. You'll be glad you have it!

TECHNO NERD TEACHES...

This icon gives you technical information that you can use to blow the minds of your friends and colleagues (and then forget five minutes later).

Kudos, Huzzahs, and Miscellaneous Plaudits

Oscar Wilde once said that a writer "can survive everything but a misprint." So it's a good thing we have editors to dot our i's and cross our t's, or most of us wouldn't get past our first book! This is especially true of the good folks at Alpha Books, who, besides being a lot of fun to work with, have taken quality editing and production to new heights.

Many people had a hand or two in the making of this book (there's a list of them all near the front of the book), but there are a few I'd like to point out in particular. Special thanks go to Publisher Marie Butler-Knight, Acquisitions Editor Barry Pruett, Development Editor Mary Rack, Copy Editor San Dee Phillips, Production Editor Michelle Shaw, and Technical Editor Herb Feltner.

I'd also like to thank my friends and family who always seem to forgive me for calling less often when I'm in the throes of a book.

Trademarks

All terms mentioned in this book that are known to be trademarks or service marks are listed below. In addition, terms suspected of being trademarks or service marks have been appropriately capitalized. Alpha Books cannot attest to the accuracy of this information. Use of a term in this book should not be regarded as affecting the validity of any trademark or service mark.

Microsoft Access, Microsoft Windows, and Microsoft DOS are registered trademarks of Microsoft Corporation.

PC Paintbrush is a registered trademark of ZSoft Corporation.

CorelDRAW! is a registered trademark of Corel Corporation.

Part I
Feel the Fear and Do It Anyway: Getting Started with Access

Microsoft Access is one of those behemoth programs that seems designed, at first glance, only to intimidate the heck out of us. I mean, one look at all those installation disks and the umpteen manuals is enough to send even the hardiest individual into cardiac arrest. The good news is that things are not as bad as they seem. The secret is to become familiar with a few (relatively) painless basics, and that's what the chapters here in Part I are designed to do. I'll be giving you some background on what databases are and why we have to suffer through them, then you'll move on to things like starting Access, getting comfy with your mouse and keyboard, and how to use the Access menus, toolbars, and dialog boxes to make your life easier. Finally, you'll put it all together and create a database, just to prove you really can do it, and to whet your appetite for things to come. It's all quite civil, really, and at the end of it all, you'll be set for the rest of your Access life.

Chapter 1
Top 10 Things You Need to Know

In a hurry? Got a date and you can't be late? No problem. For the perpetually harried in the audience, this chapter presents abridged versions of the 10 most common Access tasks. We'll cover things like starting and quitting Access, creating a table, entering and sorting data, and saving and printing a table. The steps listed here will get you up and running quickly so you can get your work done and then move on to the next crisis. Of course, I cover each of these topics in depth elsewhere in the book. I'll let you know the relevant sections as we go along so, when you've got more time on your hands (hah!), you can refer to the appropriate section for a more leisurely read.

1. Starting Access

For my money, one of *the* secrets to figuring out all this computer monkey business is to follow the old adage "first things first." If you take things step-by-step and try not to get ahead of yourself, you'll come out smelling like a rose 99 times out of 100. So, in that spirit, let's begin at the beginning and see how you start Access.

I'm assuming here that you've already installed Access. If you haven't, check out the "Installing Access" section near the end of the book to get the poop on the installation procedure.

Since Access is a Windows application, you first need to start Windows if you haven't already. You do this from the DOS prompt (the **C:\>** or **C>** thing) by typing **win** and pressing **Enter**. Once Windows cranks itself up to speed, open the program group that contains the Microsoft Access icon, as shown below. (The name of this group depends on which group you specified during the installation process. If you're not sure, try any of the following possibilities: **Microsoft Office, Access, Applications,** or **Programs**.) The easiest way to do this is to hold down the **Alt** key, press **w**, release **Alt**, and then use the up and down arrow keys to select the program group from the bottom of the menu.

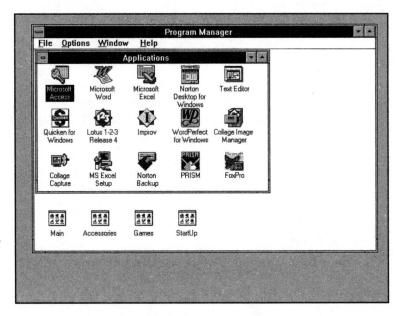

You start Access by selecting the Microsoft Access icon thingy in one of your Program Manager groups.

If you have a mouse, double-click on the **Microsoft Access** icon ("double-clicking" means that you position the mouse pointer over the icon and then quickly press the left mouse button twice in succession). If you're using a keyboard, use the arrow keys to highlight the icon, and then press **Enter**. Access will now start.

To learn more about starting Access, see Chapter 3, "Where Angels Fear to Tread: Getting Started with Access." This chapter also gives you the scoop on using the keyboard and mouse with Access. To get properly acquainted with pull-down menus, see Chapter 4, "Making Access Do Something: Menu and Toolbar Basics."

2. Creating a Database

Chapter 2, "Databases: A Painless Primer," introduces you to database fundamentals. For now, though, it's enough to know that a *database* is a file where you store data (such as customer names and addresses). It is, as you can imagine, what Access is all about.

To create a new database, pull down the File menu (by pressing **Alt+F**), and select the New Database command. Access displays a dialog box named New Database and suggests a name for the file (for example, if this is your first database, Access suggests the name **db1.mdb**). If you'd like to use something different, enter a name that is no more than eight characters long. When you're ready, click on **OK**, or press **Enter**.

You can also display the New Database dialog box by pressing **Ctrl+N**.

Chapter 3, "Where Angels Fear to Tread: Getting Started with Access," gives more in-depth info on creating and naming a database.

3. Opening an Existing Database

Rare is the database that is used once and discarded. In fact, you'll probably find that you make regular use of most of the databases you create. For example, a database of your household possessions will need to be updated after each shopping spree. Similarly, a database of business transactions will probably require modifications daily.

To use a previously created database, you need to *open* it. You do this by first pulling down the File menu and then selecting the Open Database command. This displays the Open Database dialog box. To select a file from the list, press **Tab**, and then use the up and down arrow keys to highlight the name of the database you want to open. When you're ready, you can either select the **OK** button or press **Enter** to open the file.

Pressing **Ctrl+O** also displays the Open Database dialog box.

Chapter 3 contains the gory details of opening an existing database. To learn more about navigating in a dialog box, such as Open Database, see Chapter 5, "Talking to the Access Dialog Boxes."

4. Creating a Table

In Access, a *table* is a container that holds the database information. It's like an electronic equivalent of a business card file or recipe box. Each table is divided into one or more *fields* that contain a specific type of data (such as a name, address, or ingredients list). When you create a table, you tell Access the names of the fields and what kind of information the field will contain.

To create a table in the currently open database, you first pull down the File menu, select the New command, and then select the Table command. In the New Table dialog box that appears, select the New Table button. Access displays a Table window similar to the one shown below. For each field you want to include in the table, you need to do three things:

Access includes a nifty Table Wizard feature that can take the pain out of creating certain kinds of tables. See Chapter 8 to find out more.

☞ In the Field Name column, enter a name for the field.

☞ In the Data Type column, use the drop-down list (hold down **Alt**, and press the down arrow key; see Chapter 5 to learn how to use drop-down lists) to select the type of data that will appear in the field.

☞ In the Description field, enter a brief description of the field.

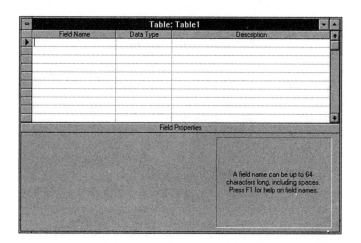

An empty Access table just itching for you to add new fields.

When you're done, select the Close command from the File menu, and then select Yes when Access asks if you want to save changes. In the Save As dialog box, enter a name for the table, and then select **OK**, or press **Enter**. If Access asks you about something called a *primary key*, ignore it for now (by selecting **No**).

Look at Chapter 8, "Creating a Table Using the Handy Table Wizard," and Chapter 9, "Creating a Table with Your Bare Hands" for unexpurgated coverage of table creation.

5. Entering Table Data

Databases, of course, aren't good for much until you enter some data. In Access, you enter data by filling in the various fields in a *datasheet* that is associated with each table. To display the datasheet, you first need to highlight the table you want to work with. You do that by selecting the Table tab in the Database window (you can either click on the tab with your mouse or else select the Tables command from the View menu) and then using the up or down arrow keys to highlight the table, as shown in the next figure. With the table name highlighted, you can either double-click on the name, select the Open button, or press **Enter**. The datasheet appears.

Open a table's datasheet by first highlighting the table name in the Database window and then double-clicking on the name or pressing Enter.

Once you have the datasheet opened, you enter data simply by typing the appropriate information under each field heading. Each line in the datasheet is called a *record*, and it represents a single item in the database (such as a recipe or contact). When you're done, select Close from the File menu.

See Chapter 10, "Setting the Table: Entering Table Data," to learn more about Access data entry. To learn how to customize the datasheet to suit your needs, take a peek at Chapter 11, "Gaining the Upper Hand on Those Pesky Datasheets." Finally, for easy data entry, Access includes a handy little item called a *form*. See Chapters 12 and 13 to get more info.

6. Finding Data

Once you get the hang of the data entry thing, you may end up with tables containing dozens or even hundreds of records. As impressive as these large databases are, it can often be a nightmare trying to find the information you want (you never know when you'll need to get your hands on that Peanut Butter and Jelly Casserole recipe). To help out, Access includes a Find feature that will sniff out a word or phrase from any field in the table and then display the appropriate record on-screen.

To use this feature, open the table and place the cursor inside the field you want to use for the search (use **Tab** or **Shift+Tab** to move between fields). Then pull down the Edit menu and select the Find command to display the Find in field dialog box. Use the Find What box to enter the word or phrase you want to find, and then select the Find Next button. If Access finds a match, it highlights the record.

The Find feature has a number of options that can make it easier to find the data you want. To get the lowdown on these options, check out Chapter 14, "The Needle in a Haystack Thing: Finding and Sorting Data."

A quick way to get the Find feature started is to press **Ctrl+F**.

7. Sorting Data

Another way to make a large table easier to manage is to *sort* the records by a particular field. For example, if you have a table of clients, you might want to sort the table by last name or company name. Or if you were planning a trip to, say, Terre Haute, you could sort the table by city and display all the Terre Haute records to make sure you don't miss anyone.

To sort a table, first place the cursor inside the field you want to use for the sort. Then pull down the Records menu, select Quick Sort, and then select either Ascending (to sort from 0 to 9 and A to Z) or Descending (Z to A and 9 to 0).

Chapter 14, "The Needle in a Haystack Thing: Finding and Sorting Data," tells you more about sorting Access tables.

8. Saving a Table

If a power failure or some other disaster should hit while you're entering data, you could lose all your precious information and have to start over. To avoid this most unpleasant fate, you should save your work regularly. When the datasheet is open, all you do is pull down the File menu and select the Save command. Access saves a copy of the table to the relatively safe confines of your computer's hard disk.

To make saving even easier (so you'll be more likely to do it often), Access also lets you simply press **Ctrl+S**.

For some extra info on saving, see Chapter 10, "Setting the Table: Entering Table Data."

When displaying the Print dialog box, you can bypass the pull-down menus altogether by simply pressing **Ctrl+P**.

9. Printing a Table

Many people like to keep a printout of their table data, just in case their computer goes up in flames (no, it doesn't happen all *that* often). To do this (get a printout I mean, not make your computer burst into flames), turn on your printer, and then open the table you want to print. Now select the Print command from the File menu. In the Print dialog box that appears, use the Copies box to select the number of copies you want printed, then select **OK** or press **Enter**.

Printing is pretty straightforward, but there are a few other tricks you might want to know (such as how to get a preview of your printout). You can get the full scoop in Chapter 11, "Gaining the Upper Hand on Those Pesky Datasheets."

You can also quit Access by pressing **Alt+F4**.

10. Quitting Access

When you've had just about enough of Access and you want to move on to more important things (such as finishing that game of Solitaire), you can quit the program by selecting the Exit command from the File menu.

Chapter 2
Databases: A Painless Primer

In This Chapter

- ☛ What is a database?
- ☛ How database software makes things easier
- ☛ Some database terms to get familiar with
- ☛ How Access fits in to all this
- ☛ The author, previously in denial, owns up to his utter lack of organizational skills

Before throwing yourself into the deep end of the Access pool, it's probably a good idea to dip a toe or two into the water so you'll be more prepared for the ordeal to come. This chapter does just that by taking a short, nontechnical look at what databases are, what you can do with them, and what Access can do for you. Shoes off!

So Just What the Heck Is a Database, Anyway?

Of all the geeky computer terms we're forced to slog through day after day, *database* is one of the easiest for us mere mortals to understand. Why? Well, simply because we use databases in one form or another every day of our lives. For example, what do the following things have in common: the yellow pages; a recipe box; a TV guide; a library; your brain? Right: they're all organized collections of information.

SPEAK LIKE A GEEK

A **database** is any organized collection of information.

What's my point? Simply that an "organized collection of information" is exactly what a database is. The yellow pages is a database of company names, addresses, and phone numbers; a recipe box is a database of—you guessed it—recipes; a TV guide is a database of this week's TV shows; and a library is a database of books and magazines. Your brain is a database of memories, instincts, and who knows what else (although, I must say, calling *my* brain an "organized" collection is, at best, a stretch).

You Say Day-tuh and I Say Dah-tuh . . .

In computer lingo, any kind of information is called *data*. Data is what computers eat for breakfast; it's the fodder that makes our programs run and justifies our typically outlandish expenditures on these hulking brutes.

Data comes in many forms: plain text, stock quotes, bank account balances, and so on. A computer program typically either reads this data from some external source (such as a floppy disk) or else asks you to enter it manually. In either case, once the data has been captured, the typically narrow-minded and autocratic software we normally have to put up with usually stores it in some fixed format and only gives us a limited number of ways to view or work with the information.

Database Software to the Rescue!

The data democrats of the computer world are database programs such as Access. Their reason for being is to free your data from its shackles so you can easily extract the information you need and manipulate the data to your heart's content.

A computer database, like its real-world counterparts, is also an organized collection of information. The difference is that the structure of a computer database allows it to be more flexible. For example, to find a phone number in an address book, you usually have to know the person's last name. Most address books are organized by name, and there's no way to change that once an address book has been set up that way. If the same address book existed in a computer database, however, you'd be able to search for a listing by address, by first name, or even by zip code.

Similarly, computer databases also let you easily change the order of the data. Your regular address book may be listed by last name, but its computer equivalent can easily show the various entries in order of, say, city or state. You can also display subsets of the data. Sociable types may have a few hundred or more people in their address books. With a computer database, you can narrow down the displayed entries to show only the people with, say, the first name Monty who live in Truth or Consequences, New Mexico.

Some Database Terms You Need to Know

Databases, like all computer subjects, have their own unique terminology. Fortunately, *unlike* most computer subjects, much of the basic database jargon is mirrored in real life. Although I'll be explaining most database terms as they arise, I'd like to introduce a few here that are crucial if you hope to get the most out of Access:

field   A single category of information. For example, a database of addresses might have the following six fields: name, address, city, state, zip code, phone number.

field name   The name of the field, such as Address or City (this is not rocket science). You use the field name to refer to the field in various database operations.

record   A single entry in the database. In our address book example, a record would consist of a single person's name, address, city, state, zip code, and phone number.

How Does Access Fit Into All This?

Access knows databases. In fact, Access is so adept at this database stuff that the pocket-protector crowd calls it a *database management system*. Now that sure sounds impressive, but what the heck does it mean? Well, it's nothing mysterious: it simply means that Access not only stores your information in a database, but it also supplies you with the means to manage (sort, search, extract, and so on) this information.

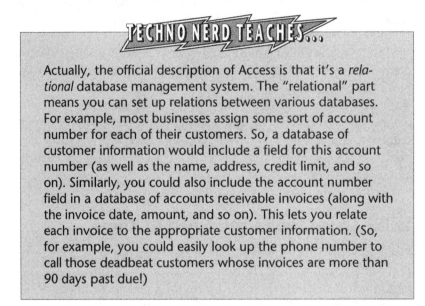

TECHNO NERD TEACHES...

Actually, the official description of Access is that it's a *relational* database management system. The "relational" part means you can set up relations between various databases. For example, most businesses assign some sort of account number for each of their customers. So, a database of customer information would include a field for this account number (as well as the name, address, credit limit, and so on). Similarly, you could also include the account number field in a database of accounts receivable invoices (along with the invoice date, amount, and so on). This lets you relate each invoice to the appropriate customer information. (So, for example, you could easily look up the phone number to call those deadbeat customers whose invoices are more than 90 days past due!)

However, Access is not your average, run-of-the-mill database management system, no sir. It takes a unique approach to the subject that, once you get used to it (which is not long), is certainly convenient and possibly even intuitive. To see why Access is unique, we need to re-examine databases from the Access perspective.

Access Databases: Something a Little Different

Until now, I've presented a database as a collection of data with some sort of underlying organization. In most systems, anything related to the data (such as a data entry screen or a slick-looking report that summarizes the data) is considered a separate piece of the overall pie. Access, though, is different because its databases consist not only of the basic data, but also related items you use to work with the data.

I like to think of an Access database as a kind of electronic toolshed. In this toolshed, you have not only your raw materials (your data) stored in bins and containers of various shapes and sizes, but you also have a number of tools you can use to manipulate these materials, as well as a work area where all the fun happens.

Each Access database can contain four different types of objects: tables, forms, queries, and reports. (For the sake of accuracy, there are also two other kinds of objects you can include in an Access database: macros and modules. These are advanced tools that computer gurus use to build their own Access applications. For the rest of us, they just make our heads hurt, so I won't cover them in this book.)

SPEAK LIKE A GEEK

In Access lingo, tables, forms, queries, and reports are called **objects**.

Tables: Containers for Your Data

As one of the most disorganized people on the face of the earth, I can attest to the power of databases to simplify and order your life. For example, I'm constantly writing down people's names, phone numbers, and even addresses in random locations: on sticky-notes, scraps of paper, my desk calendar, or other people's business cards. A computer database allows me (when I'm in one of my rare "get organized" moods) to record all this

haphazard information in a single, easily accessible location (and saves me from having to decipher my hasty chicken scratches jotted during the heat of a telephone call).

In Access databases, you store your information in an object called a *table*. Tables are rectangular arrangements of rows and columns, where each column represents a field (that is, a specific category of information), and each row represents a record (a single entry in the table).

As the next two pictures show, you just take your raw data and transfer it into an Access table. Notice how the table includes separate fields (columns) for each logical grouping of the data (first name, last name, address, city, and so on).

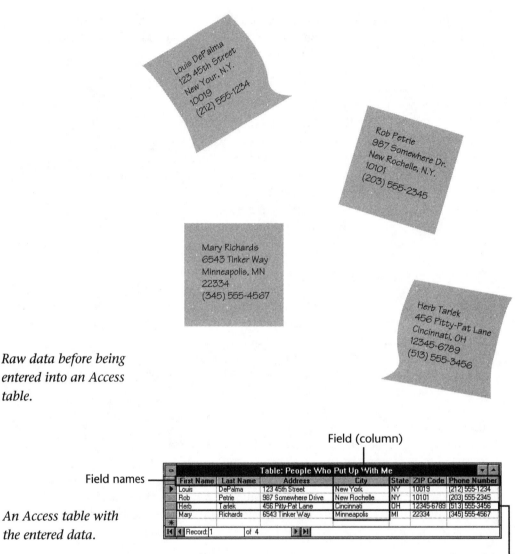

Raw data before being entered into an Access table.

Field (column)

Field names —

An Access table with the entered data.

First Name	Last Name	Address	City	State	ZIP Code	Phone Number
Louis	DePalma	123 45th Street	New York	NY	10019	(212) 555-1234
Rob	Petrie	987 Somewhere Drive	New Rochelle	NY	10101	(203) 555-2345
Herb	Tarlek	456 Pitty-Pat Lane	Cincinnati	OH	12345-6789	(513) 555-3456
Mary	Richards	6543 Tinker Way	Minneapolis	MI	22334	(345) 555-4567

Table: People Who Put Up With Me

Record: 1 of 4

Record (row)

See Chapter 8, "Creating a Table Using the Handy Table Wizard," and Chapter 9, "Creating a Table with Your Bare Hands," to learn how to create tables and stuff them full of data.

Forms: Making Data Entry Easier

Entering data into a table is unglamorous at best, and downright mind-numbing at worst. To make this chore easier, you can create Access database objects called *forms*. Forms provide you with a *template* that you fill in whenever you enter a record. The form displays a blank box for each field in the table, and data entry becomes a simple matter of filling in the appropriate boxes. As you can see in the following sample form, each box is labeled so you always know what type of data you're entering. Best of all, each form is easily customizable, so you can move the fields around to make them look like real-life forms, and you can add fancy effects, such as graphics, to give your forms pizzazz.

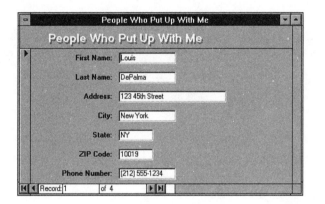

You can use Access forms to make data entry easier.

Check out Chapter 12, "Using Forms for Easy-As-Pie Data Entry," and Chapter 13, "Improving Your Form," to learn more about using Access forms.

Queries: Asking Questions of Your Data

By far, the most common concern expressed by new database users (and many old-timers, as well) is how to extract the information you need from all that data. If you only need to look up a phone number or address, Access has powerful search capabilities (which I'll cover in Chapter 13, "The Needle in a Haystack Thing: Finding and Sorting Data").

But what if, for example, you have a database of accounts receivable invoices and your boss wants to know *right away* how many invoices are more than 150 days past due? You could try counting the appropriate records, but if the database is a large one, you'd probably be out of a job before you finished counting. The better way would be to ask Access to do the counting for you by creating another type of database object: a *query*. Queries are, literally, questions you ask of your data. In this case, you could ask Access to display a list of all invoices more than 150 days past due.

Queries let you extract from one or more tables a subset of the data. For example, in my database of names and addresses, what if I wanted to see a list of those people from New York state? No problem. I'd just set up the following query: "Which records have "NY" in the State field?" The answer to this question is shown in the next figure.

The answer to an Access query that asked the musical question "Which people in the table are from New York state?"

To get the scoop on queries, turn to Part IV, "Ask and Ye Shall Receive: Querying Access Tables."

Reports: Making Your Data Look Good

Even though tables are decidedly neater than sticky-notes and scraps of paper, the information is still "raw," in that it appears in a rather dull and unpolished row-and-column format. To make your data more palatable for others to read, you can create a fourth type of database object: a *report*. Reports let you define how you want your data to appear on the printed page. You can decide which fields to include in the report, where they appear on the page, which font to use (that is, the size and shape of the characters), and you can also add your own text and graphics. Best of all, reports are easy to generate, although people will think you spent 10 times longer working on the report than you actually did.

Access has a number of predefined report styles to make things even easier. For example, the following report uses the names and addresses from my sample database to create mailing labels. You can create a similar report with only a few mouse clicks.

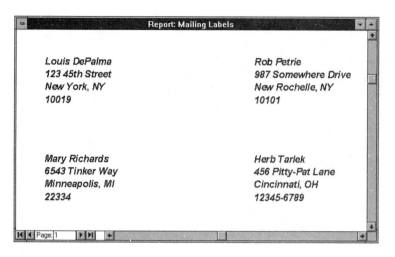

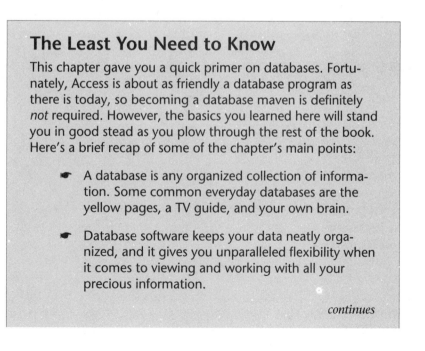

A sample report that generates mailing labels.

   The two chapters in Part V, "Impressing Friends and Family with Access Reports," tell you everything you need to know about creating and working with reports.

The Least You Need to Know

This chapter gave you a quick primer on databases. Fortunately, Access is about as friendly a database program as there is today, so becoming a database maven is definitely *not* required. However, the basics you learned here will stand you in good stead as you plow through the rest of the book. Here's a brief recap of some of the chapter's main points:

- ☛ A database is any organized collection of information. Some common everyday databases are the yellow pages, a TV guide, and your own brain.

- ☛ Database software keeps your data neatly organized, and it gives you unparalleled flexibility when it comes to viewing and working with all your precious information.

continues

continued

☞ In computer databases, a field is a category of information, a field name is the name you use to refer to the field in database operations, and a record is a single entry in the database.

☞ Access is a database management system that gives you many tools to enter, edit, and manage your data.

☞ Access databases can contain four types of objects: tables, forms, queries, and reports.

Chapter 3

Where Angels Fear to Tread: Getting Started with Access

In This Chapter

☞ Starting Windows

☞ Learning about the mouse

☞ Learning about the keyboard

☞ Starting and quitting Access

☞ Rodent wrestling and other bizarre skills of the computer age

After all that theory in Chapter 2, I feel an urge for some good old-fashioned practical know-how. That's what you'll get in this chapter as I show you how to get started with Access. I'll begin by showing you how to start Windows, then I'll give you some brief lessons on using the mouse and keyboard, and then we'll load Access to see what all the fuss is about. If you're ready (a few deep breaths might help at this point), then we'll begin. . . .

First Things First: Starting Windows

Access is a Windows application, which means that Windows has to be running before you can start Access. If Windows is already loaded, you can read the next few paragraphs if you're feeling gung ho, but I hereby give you permission to skip ahead to the "Wrestling with the Mouse" section.

Not sure if Windows is running? Okay, here are two sure-fire clues:

☞ Your screen is mostly blank, except for something that looks like **C:\>** or **C>**. This means you're definitely *not* in Windows.

☞ Your screen contains a box that says **Program Manager** at the top. This means you definitely *are* in Windows.

BY THE WAY

With Windows started, you should now see a box on your screen that says **Program Manager** at the top. If you don't, find the nearest guru and tell her that some dork in a book wants you to be in Program Manager. Better yet, why not learn how to do it yourself by picking up a copy of *The Complete Idiot's Guide to Windows* by the same dork? (Ah, yes, that *was* a shameless plug, wasn't it?)

Finding the DOS Prompt

You need to be at the DOS prompt to start Windows. If you've never seen a DOS prompt, examine your screen for something that looks like C:\> or C> or any variation of these. If there is no prompt, then you're probably in some other program. Here are some possibilities:

☞ The MS-DOS Shell program. If you see **MS-DOS Shell** at the top of your screen, hold down the **Alt** key, and press **F4** to return to DOS.

☞ Some kind of menu system. Your computer may be set up with a menu system that gives you a list of programs to run. If one of those programs is Windows, then you're in luck! Go ahead and select the appropriate option to start Windows. Otherwise, look for an option called **Exit to DOS** or **Quit** or something similar. You can also try pressing the **Esc** key.

The Two-Step Program for Starting Windows

Without further ado, here are the steps you need to follow to get Windows up and running:

1. If necessary, change to the drive on which you installed Windows by typing the drive letter and a colon (:) and pressing the **Enter** key. For example, to change to drive C, type **c:** and press **Enter**.

2. Type **win** and press **Enter** to start Windows loading (yes, it does seem to take forever to load).

Before learning how to start Access, let's take a few moments to tackle some mouse and keyboard basics. You'll thank me in the end.

Wrestling with the Mouse

Learning how to use a mouse just might be your most important Access survival skill. Why? Well, because most of Access is designed with the mouse in mind, so you'll find it makes many everyday tasks just plain faster and easier. Luckily, using a mouse takes no extraordinary physical skills. If you can cut your own food, then you'll have no trouble wielding a mouse. (If you don't have a mouse, what are you doing reading this? Skip ahead to the section called "Access Keyboarding for Non-Typists.")

A mouse is a marvelous little mechanical miracle that can seem incomprehensible to the uninitiated. The basic idea, though, is simple: you move the mouse on its pad or on your desk, and a small arrow moves correspondingly on the screen. By positioning the arrow on strategic screen areas, you can select objects, open database tables, and alter the shape and size of windows. Not bad for a rodent!

The arrow that moves on your screen when you move a mouse is called the **mouse pointer.**

The Basic Mouse Technique

Using a mouse is straightforward, but it does take some getting used to. Here is the basic technique:

1. Turn the mouse so that its cable extends away from you.

2. Place your hand over the mouse in such a way that:

   ☞ The part of the mouse nearest you nestles snugly in the palm of your hand.

   ☞ Your index and middle fingers rest lightly on the two mouse buttons (if your mouse has three buttons, rest your fingers on the two outside buttons).

☞ Your thumb and ring finger hold the mouse gently on either side.

3. Move the mouse around on its pad or on your desk. Notice how the mouse pointer on the screen moves in the same direction as the mouse itself.

The Hard Part: Controlling the Darn Thing!

Moving the mouse pointer is simple enough, but *controlling* the pesky little thing is another matter. Most new mouse users complain that the pointer seems to move erratically, or that they move to one part of the screen and run out of room to maneuver. To help out, here are a few tips that will get you well on your way to becoming a veritable mouse maven:

☞ Don't grab the mouse as if you were going to throw it across the room (although you may, on occasion, be tempted to do this). A light touch is all you need.

☞ The distance the mouse pointer travels on the screen depends on how quickly you move the mouse. If you move the mouse very slowly for about an inch, the pointer moves about the same distance (a little more, actually). However, if you move the mouse very fast for about an inch, the pointer leaps across the screen.

☞ If you find yourself at the edge of the mouse pad but the pointer isn't where you want it to be, simply pick up the mouse and move it to the middle of the pad. This doesn't affect the position of the pointer, but it does allow you to continue on your way.

Mouse Actions

Throughout this book, I'll be asking you to take certain actions with the mouse. Here's a list of those actions and the words I'll be using to identify them:

Point   This means you move the mouse pointer so that it rests on a specific screen location.

Click   This means you quickly press and release the left mouse button. For example, if I say something like "click on the green and purple doodad," it means you first point at the green and purple doodad and then click the button.

Right-click   This is the same as clicking, except you do it with the *right* mouse button. (If your mouse has three buttons, use the one on the far right.)

Double-click   As you might expect, *double-*clicking means you quickly press and release the left mouse button *twice* in succession. This can be a bit tricky until you get the rhythm, sort of like learning a dance-step. Again, you'll always first point at something before you double-click.

Drag   This has nothing to do with dressing funny. It simply means that you press and *hold down* the left mouse button and then move the mouse.

BY THE WAY

If you'd like to improve your mouse skills *and* have some fun in the process, check out the Solitaire game that comes free with Windows. To start Solitaire, first double-click on Program Manager's **Games** icon to open the Games window. Now double-click on the **Solitaire** icon. Here's a summary of the mouse actions you'll be using to play the game:

- ☛ Click on the deck to deal more cards.

- ☛ Drag the cards to move them between the row stacks.

- ☛ Double-click on a card to place it on the suit stack.

Access Keyboarding for Non-Typists

Although a mouse is handy for many Access tasks, it's by no means essential. In fact, many Access commands have built-in keyboard shortcuts that can be real time-savers. Does this mean you have to become some kind of expert typist to use Access? Hardly. I've been using computer keyboards for years, and I wouldn't know what touch typing was if it bit me in the face.

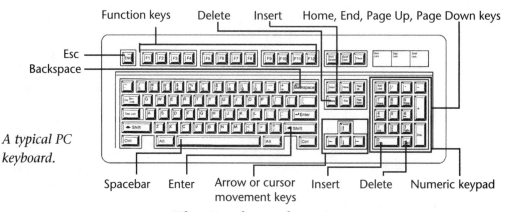

Function keys   Delete   Insert   Home, End, Page Up, Page Down keys

Esc

Backspace

A typical PC keyboard.

Spacebar   Enter   Arrow or cursor   Insert   Delete   Numeric keypad
movement keys

The Keyboard Layout

Since it's so much work to say something like "hold down the **x** key, press the **y** key, and then release **x**," in this book, I'll abbreviate all such key combinations with the simpler phrase "press **x+y**." So, for example, I'd abbreviate the key combination that displays the Task List as follows: "press **Ctrl+Esc**."

Although there are almost as many keyboard styles as there are keyboard manufacturers, they all share a few features. In particular, all keyboards are divided into three sections: an alphanumeric keypad, a numeric keypad, and a function keypad, as you can see here.

Using the Alphanumeric Keypad

The alphanumeric keypad is the section of the keyboard that contains the letters, punctuation marks, and other special characters that you use most often (and some, like ~ and ^, that *nobody* uses). This section also contains several other keys that you use to execute Access commands and functions, including the Ctrl, Alt, and Shift keys. Generally, you don't use these keys by themselves but as part of *key combinations*.

For example, try holding down the **Ctrl** key, pressing the **Esc** key, and then releasing **Ctrl**. This causes the Windows Task List to pop up on your screen. This method of holding down one key while pressing another is called a *key combination* and is used extensively in Access. (By the way, to remove the Task List, just press **Esc** by itself.)

Using the Numeric Keypad

On each type of keyboard, the numeric keypad serves two functions. When the Num Lock key is on, you can use the numeric keypad to enter numbers. If Num Lock is off, the keypad cursor keys (the left and right arrow keys, the up and down arrow keys, Page Up, Page Down, Home, and End) are enabled, and you can use these to navigate a window or table. Some keyboards (called *extended* keyboards) have a separate cursor keypad so you can keep Num Lock on all the time.

I'm assuming here that you've installed Access (or conned someone else into doing it for you). If not, go directly to the last section in this book and turn to "Installing Access." Do not pass Go, do not collect $200.

Using the Function Keys

The function keys are located either to the left of the alphanumeric keypad or across the top of the keyboard, and on some keyboards there's a set in each location. There are usually 12 function keys (although some older keyboards have only 10), and they're labeled F1, F2, and so on. In Access, you use these keys either by themselves or as part of key combinations. See the "Quitting Access" section at the end of this chapter for an example.

Starting Access

All right, it's time to get down to brass tacks and start Access. Here are the easy steps to follow:

1. Hold down the **Alt** key on your keyboard, and then tap **W**. You'll see a menu of options appear. The numbered options at the bottom of the menu are names of your *program groups*.

2. Look for the name of the program group where you installed Access. If you're not sure, look for any of the following names: **Microsoft Office**, **Applications**, **Programs**, or **Access**. Press the number you see beside the program group name. This displays the program group, and you should see a picture named **Microsoft Access**. If you don't, you'll need to select a different group.

Select this little fellow to start Access.

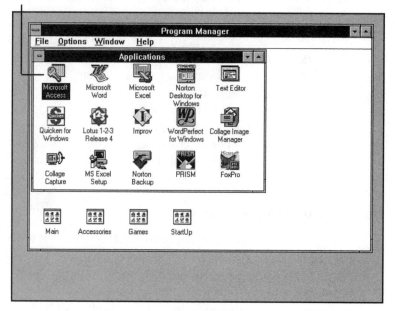

Look for a program group that contains the Microsoft Access picture.

3. You start Access by "selecting" the Microsoft Access picture, like so:

    With a mouse, double-click on the picture.

    OR

    With your keyboard, press the arrow keys until the picture is highlighted, and then press **Enter**.

The boxes you see (such as Program Manager and Applications) are called windows. The little pictures you see infesting Program Manager's boxes are called icons.

Checking Out the Access Screen

When Access loads, you'll see a screen similar to the one shown here. Kind of disappointing isn't it? I mean, after installing all those disks *this* is all we get? Sheesh!

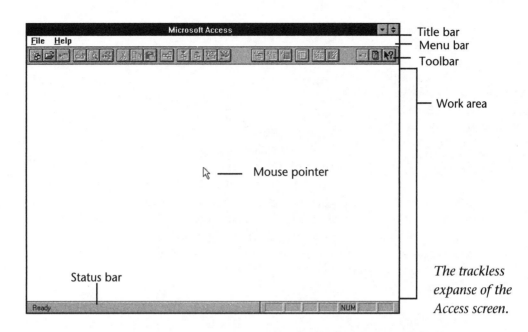

The trackless expanse of the Access screen.

However, as barren as the initial screen looks, it's not totally empty. Here's a list of the few things that break up the monotony:

Title bar   This is the top line of the screen, and it tells you that you're in Microsoft Access (in case you mistake it for the Mojave desert or something, I suppose).

Menu bar   This is the second line of the screen, and it contains the Access *pull-down menus*. These menus contain the commands you use to run all of the Access functions and features. You'll learn about these menus in Chapter 4, "Making Access Do Something: Menu and Toolbar Basics."

Toolbar   This handy little item provides mouse users with a shortcut method for running Access' most frequently used commands. You'll find everything you need to know about your toolbar in Chapter 4.

Work area   This is the massive, blank expanse below the toolbar. This is where all the Access action happens.

Status bar   This is the bottom line of the screen. Access uses this area mostly to provide you with messages about what its commands do and what the program is currently up to. For example, the status bar displays **Ready** when you first load Access. This means that Access is waiting patiently for you do to something.

An easier way to exit Access is to press **Alt+F4**. This bypasses the menu altogether and takes you right out of the program.

Quitting Access

I know, I know. You haven't even done anything yet, and here I am telling you to quit the program. Well, you have to do it sometime, so you may as well know the drill. Besides, it's easy as pie. You begin by pressing the **Alt+F** key combination. This displays a menu of commands (yes, it's one of those pull-down menus we talked about earlier), most of which will seem incomprehensible (which is perfectly normal at this early stage of your Access career). Fortunately, you can ignore most of them. The only one you need to deal with is the Exit command at the bottom of the menu. Select this command by either clicking on it with your mouse or by pressing the **X** key. Access quits and returns you to Program Manager.

The Least You Need to Know

This chapter got you started on the Access bandwagon with some basic techniques you'll be using every day. Here's the highlight film:

- ☞ Access is a Windows application, so you need to start Windows (by typing **win** and pressing **Enter** at the DOS prompt) before you do anything else.

- ☞ For easier Access access, become friends with your mouse.

- ☞ To start Access, select the **Microsoft Access** icon from the appropriate program group in Program Manager.

- ☞ To quit Access, select the Exit command from the File menu, or press **Alt+F4**.

Chapter 4
Making Access Do Something: Menu and Toolbar Basics

In This Chapter

- What are pull-down menus?
- How to use pull-down menus with a mouse
- How to use pull-down menus with the keyboard
- Using the Access toolbars
- Rambling ruminations on desks, drawers, and hieroglyphics

When they start Access for the first time, the question that pops immediately into most people's minds is "Now what?" When you load your word processor, you can start typing without further ado. Same with your spreadsheet; you just crank it up and start entering numbers. With Access, though, you just get that intimidating blank screen. You can slam most of the keys on your keyboard until you're blue in the face, and the dumb beast will just sit there, mocking your efforts.

To make Access do something, you need to know about *pull-down menus* and *toolbars*. These features are your gateway to all of the Access commands and functions, and they're the subject of this chapter.

So Just What Is a Pull-Down Menu, Anyway?

Take a good look at the desk you're sitting at. (If you're not sitting at a desk, picturing one in your head will do.) You probably have an area where you do your work, surrounded by various tools (pens, pencils, and so on) and things that keep you informed (such as a clock and calendar). You probably also see a few drawers, from which you get your work and in which you store your desk tools.

The Access screen is also a lot like a desk. You have the work area, of course, and you have the status bar to keep you informed. And you also have the menu bar's *pull-down menus* that work, in fact, just like desk drawers. When you need to get more work (that is, open a database) or run an Access feature, you simply open the appropriate menu and select the menu option that runs the feature.

Why You Pull Down Instead of Up or Out

Why are they called "pull-down" menus? Well, because they're hidden inside the menu bar near the top of the screen. Selecting any of the menu bar options (at first you only see two: File and Help, but others will appear as you work with different parts of Access) displays a menu of choices, such as the File menu shown here.

The effect, you'll note, is as though you pulled the menu down from the menu bar. See, sometimes this stuff actually makes sense!

```
┌──────────────────────────────────────────────────────────────┐
│ ⊟                     Microsoft Access                    ▼│▲ │
├──────────────────────────────────────────────────────────────┤
│ File  Help                                                   │
├─────────────────────────────┐                                │
│ New Database...      Ctrl+N  │◢▢◣◿  ◢▣◣▢▥◿    ▢◙▣?│          │
│ Open Database...     Ctrl+O  │                                │
│ Compact Database...          │                                │
│ Convert Database...          │                                │
│ Encrypt/Decrypt Database...  │                                │
│ Repair Database...           │                                │
│                              │                                │
│ Toolbars...                  │                                │
│ Unhide...                    │                                │
│ Run Macro...                 │                                │
│ Add-ins              ▶       │                                │
│                              │                                │
│ 1 HOME.MDB                   │                                │
│ 2 NWIND.MDB                  │                                │
│ 3 TEST.MDB                   │                                │
│                              │                                │
│ Exit                         │                                │
└──────────────────────────────┘                               │
│                                                              │
│                                                              │
│                                                              │
├──────────────────────────────────────────────────────────────┤
│ Create a new database             │   │   │    │NUM│  │       │
└──────────────────────────────────────────────────────────────┘
```

The File pull-down menu.

How to Use Pull-Down Menus with a Mouse

If you have a mouse, using pull-down menus is a breeze. All you do is move the mouse pointer into the menu bar area (the pointer will change to an arrow), and then click on the name of the menu you want to pull down. For example, clicking on File in the menu bar pulls down the File menu.

SPEAK LIKE A GEEK

The choices you see listed in a pull-down menu are called **commands**. You use these commands to tell Access what you want it to do next.

Once you have a menu displayed, you need to select one of the commands. This is simple enough: you just click on the command you want to execute. Depending on the option you select, one of three things will happen:

- ☛ The command will execute.

- ☛ Another menu will appear. In this case, just click on the command you want to execute from the new menu.

- ☛ Something called a "dialog box" will appear, to get further info from you. See Chapter 5, "Talking to the Access Dialog Boxes," for details on using dialog boxes.

How to Use Pull-Down Menus with the Keyboard

The secret to using pull-down menus from the keyboard is to look for the underlined letter in each menu bar option. For example, look at the "F" in File and the "H" in Help. These underlined letters are the menu option's *hot keys*. How do they work? Simple: you just hold down **Alt** and then press the designated hot key letter on your keyboard. For example, to pull down the File menu, use the **Alt+F** key combination.

If you feel **hot keys** is too racy a phrase for the underlined letters in menu options, you can also use the more sedate term **accelerator keys**.

With the menu displayed, you select a command by using the up and down arrow keys to highlight the command you want (a *highlight bar* moves up and down to mark the current command) and then press **Enter**.

As I explained in the mouse section, one of three things will happen depending on which one you select:

☛ The command will execute.

☛ Another menu will appear. In this case, use the arrow keys to select the command you want from the new menu, and then press **Enter**.

☛ A dialog box will appear, asking you for more information.

What do you do if you pull down a menu and discover you don't want to select a command? No problem. You have two choices:

☛ To return to the document, either click anywhere inside the document or press **Alt** by itself.

☛ To pull down a different menu, click on the menu name, or press **Alt** plus the letter of the new menu.

More Fun Pull-Down Menu Stuff

If you've been pulling down some menus, you may have noticed a few strange things. For example, did you notice that some commands have a triangle on the right-hand side of the menu? Or that some are followed by three ominous-looking dots? Or that others also list a key (or key combination)? These are just a few of the normal features found in all pull-down menus, and you can take advantage of them to make your life easier. The rest of this section summarizes these features. I'll be using the File menu (shown here) as an example, so you might want to pull it down now to follow along.

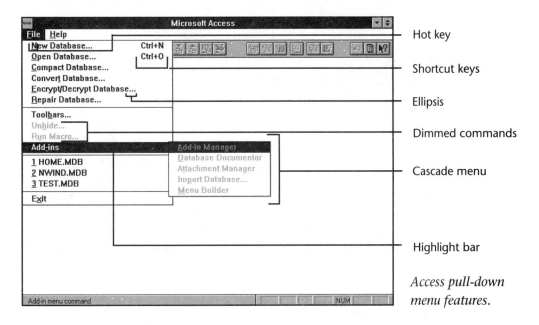

Access pull-down menu features.

Command Prompts: Helpful Hints

Access has so many commands that it's just about impossible (and probably not very useful) to remember what each one does. Fortunately, you don't have to, because whenever you highlight a command, Access displays a prompt in the status bar that gives you a brief description of the command. If this description seems reasonable, go ahead and select the command; if it doesn't, you're free to move on.

As a reminder, you highlight a command in a pulled down menu by using the up and down arrow keys to scroll through the list. Mouse users can get into the act as well, by using a slightly different technique for pulling down a menu. Move the pointer over the menu name, press the left mouse button and *hold it down*. Keep the button held down and move the mouse pointer through the menu commands. (This is called *dragging* the mouse.) As the pointer hits each command, the prompt appears in the

Yes, you heard right: to select a *command* using its hot key, you just press the key, but to select a *pull-down menu* using its hot key, you have to hold down **Alt** and then press the key. Are we confused yet?

status bar. To select a command, just release the mouse button while the command is highlighted. To remove the menu without selecting a command, move the pointer off the menu, and then release the button.

Underlined Characters: More Hot Keys

Every command in a pull-down menu has one underlined character. This means that when you display a menu, you can select any command by simply pressing its underlined letter on your keyboard. For example, in the File menu, you could select, say, the New Database command simply by pressing **N**. (If you're itching to try this out, go ahead and press **N**. You'll eventually see a box named New Database on your screen. I'll be showing you how to create a new database in Chapter 6, "Databasics: Working with Access Databases," so for now just press **Esc** to return to the Access screen.)

Shortcut Keys: The Fast Way to Work

Some menu commands also show a key or key combination on the right-hand side of the menu. These are called *shortcut keys*; they allow you to bypass the menus altogether and activate a command quickly from your keyboard. For example, you can select the File menu's New Database command simply by pressing **Ctrl+N**. (If you try this, press **Esc** to remove the New Database box that appears.)

Once you've worked with Access for a while, you may find it faster to use these shortcut keys for the commands you use most often.

Arrowheads (Menus, Menus, and More Menus)

With some commands, you'll see an arrowhead on the right side of the menu. This tells you that yet another menu will appear when you select this command. For example, if you select the Add-ins command from the File menu, you'll see a new menu appear with more commands to choose from.

Confusingly, the shortcut keys only work when you don't have a menu displayed. If you press a key combination with a menu pulled down, Access will ignore it and wait for you to do something sensible.

The Ellipsis (the Three-Dot Thing)

An *ellipsis* (...) after a command name indicates that a "dialog box" will appear when you select the option. Access uses dialog boxes to ask you for more information or to confirm a command you requested. For example, if you select the File menu's New Database command, a dialog box appears to find out what name you want to give to the new database. (Press **Esc** to remove this dialog box.) See Chapter 5, "Talking to the Access Dialog Boxes," for more dialog box details.

The extra menu that appears is called a **cascade** menu.

Check Marks: The Active Command

Some menu commands exist only to turn certain features of the program off and on (like a light switch). If a check mark appears to the left of the command, it means the feature is currently on. If you then select the command, Access turns off the feature and removes the check mark. (Unfortunately, there are no examples of check mark commands in the File menu.)

What You Can't Do: The Dimmed Commands

You'll sometimes see menu commands that appear in a lighter color than the others. These are called *dimmed commands*, and the dimming indicates that you can't select them (for now, anyway). If you see a dimmed command, it usually means you must do something else with the program before the command will become active. For example, the File menu shown earlier has two dimmed commands: Unhide and Run Macro.

Using Version 2.0's Shortcut Menus

Mouse users get an extra bonus in version 2 of Access: shortcut menus. These menus display a short list of commands related to a specific feature. All you do is place the mouse pointer over the feature and then right-click. When the menu appears, just click (the left button this time) on the command you want.

For example, if you right-click on the toolbar, you'll see this shortcut menu. All of these options are related to toolbars (which I'll discuss in the next section). To get rid of the shortcut menu, click anywhere in the work area.

One of the shortcut menus from Access version 2.

Using the Access Toolbars

Pull-down menus are a useful feature because they stay out of your way when you don't need them. However, once you've used Access for a while, you'll find there are certain commands that you select regularly. Eventually, pulling down the appropriate menus and selecting these commands several times a day will become a chore, and you'll wish there was a faster way. Well, not to worry because Access *does* provide a faster method to run a command: the *toolbar*.

The toolbar is the horizontal strip that lurks just below the menu bar. It contains a number of *buttons* that represent common Access tasks. To run the task, you simply click on the appropriate button (sorry, keyboard users; the toolbar is for mouse users only).

How do you know which button performs what task? Good question! The pictures on each button are supposed to tell you what each one does, but interpreting the buttons' arcane symbols is a task akin to deciphering ancient Egyptian hieroglyphics. To help out, Access displays cute little messages called ToolTips whenever the mouse pointer lingers over a button for a second or two. For example, place the mouse pointer over the button on the far left. After a few seconds, a yellow strip containing the words **New Database** will appear. You'll also see a message in the status bar (**Create a new database**, in this case). These two clues tell you that clicking on this button is equivalent to selecting the New Database command from the File menu.

This ToolTip identifies the New Database button.

Access actually has several different toolbars. The one you see on your screen depends on what you're doing with the program. For example, you'll see one toolbar when you're entering data into a table, and a different toolbar when you're creating a report. Happily, Access manages the toolbars for you, so you don't have to worry about which one gets displayed and when.

BY THE WAY

To make using the Access toolbars even easier, I'll point out the appropriate Version 2.0 buttons to use for each task as we go along.

The Least You Need to Know

This chapter explained the Access pull-down menus and toolbars. Here's a quick review of your newfound know-how:

- ☞ Pull-down menus are a lot like desk drawers, because they store tools (commands) that you use with Access.

- ☞ To pull down a menu with the mouse, simply click on the menu name in the menu bar.

- ☞ To pull down a menu with the keyboard, look for the menu's hot key, and then, while holding down **Alt**, press the key on your keyboard.

- ☞ Once you pull down a menu, you can select a command by using your keyboard's up and down arrow keys to highlight the command, and then pressing **Enter**. If you have a mouse, just click on the command you want.

- ☞ Shortcut menus (new in version 2) present you with a short list of commands related to a specific screen area. Right-click on the area to display its shortcut menu.

- ☞ Toolbars give you an easy way to execute the most common Access commands and features. All you do is click on the button you want.

Chapter 5
Talking to the Access Dialog Boxes

In This Chapter

- What is a dialog box?
- Getting around in dialog boxes
- Learning about dialog box buttons, boxes, and lists
- Working with scroll bars
- Odd dialog box details you might never have thought to ask about

As you work with Access, little boxes will appear on your screen incessantly, prompting you for more information (and generally just confusing the heck out of things). These are called *dialog boxes*, and they're Access' way of saying "Talk to me!" This chapter looks at these chatty little beasts, and offers some helpful tips for surviving their relentless onslaught.

Where Do They Come From?

You can always tell when a command will generate a dialog box by looking for three dots (...) after the command name. These three dots (they're known as an *ellipsis*) tell you that some kind of dialog box will appear if you select the option. This gives you time to prepare yourself mentally for the ordeal to come.

Dialog boxes may sometimes seem to appear out of nowhere, but they generally show up after you select certain commands from the pull-down menus or press certain key combinations. Whether or not a dialog box appears depends on whether or not the program needs more information from you. For example, if you select the File menu's New Database command, Access displays the New Database dialog box so you can enter a name for the new database.

Dialog Box Basics

Here are a few points about dialog boxes to keep in mind as you work through this chapter:

- ☞ Dialog boxes always have a title at the top of the box. This lets you know if you selected the right command.

- ☞ Dialog boxes like to monopolize your attention. When one is on the screen, you can't do other things, such as enter text in the typing area or select a pull-down menu. Deal with the dialog box first, and then you can move on to other things.

- ☞ The various objects you see inside a dialog box are called *controls* because you use them to control the way the dialog box works.

- ☞ Every control has a name that identifies it. Some control names will have an underlined letter that acts as the control's *hot key*. This means you can select the control by holding down the **Alt** key and pressing the letter.

Navigating Controls

Before you learn how these controls operate, you need to be able to move among them. (This section applies only to keyboard users. Mouse users select a control merely by clicking on it.)

The first thing you need to be able to figure out is which control is currently selected. (This can be easy or hard depending on how many controls the dialog box has.) You need to look for one of two things:

☛ If the control displays text inside a box, the control is active either when the text is highlighted or when you see an insertion point cursor blinking on and off inside the box.

☛ All other controls display a dotted outline around their name when they're selected.

Think of these guidelines as "You are here" signs on a map and keep them in mind as you move through the Access dialog boxes.

Once you know where you are, you can move around by pressing **Tab** (to move, more or less, top to bottom and left to right through the controls) or **Shift+Tab** (to move bottom to top and right to left).

Working with Command Buttons

The most basic dialog box control is the *command button*. The dialog box shown here has two command buttons: OK and Cancel. When you select a command button, you're telling Access to execute the command written on the face of the button.

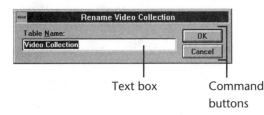

Text box   Command
              buttons

Command buttons execute the command written on their faces.

To select a command button, just click on it with the mouse. To do the same thing from the keyboard, press **Tab** until the command button you want is selected (that is, the button name is surrounded by a dotted outline), and then press **Enter**.

Access uses command buttons for all kinds of things, but two are particularly common: OK and Cancel. Here's what they do:

OK   Select this button when you've finished with the dialog box and you want to put all your selections into effect. This is the "Make it so" button.

Cancel   Select this button to cancel the dialog box. It's useful for those times when you panic and realize you're looking at the wrong dialog box, or if you've made a mess of your selections. This is the "Belay that last order" button. (You can also cancel a dialog box by pressing **Esc**.)

If you find yourself inside a dialog box and you haven't the faintest idea what to do next, press **F1**. This displays a window from the Access Help system that tells you all about the dialog box. When you're finished with Help, select **Exit** from the Help window's **File** menu to return to Access.

When the text in an text box is highlighted, it means that it will get replaced by whatever you type. If you don't want to replace the entire text, just press either the left or right arrow key to remove the highlight, and then position the insertion point appropriately.

Working with Text Boxes

A *text box* is a screen area you use to type in text information, such as a description or a file name. When you first select a text box, you'll see a blinking insertion point inside the box (if it's empty) or highlighted text (if it's not). The Rename Video Collection dialog box shown earlier contains a single text box, called Table Name.

To use a text box, click anywhere inside the box, and then type your text. If you make any mistakes when typing, you can use the **Backspace** and **Delete** keys to expunge the offending letters. To use a text box from your keyboard, press **Tab** until you see the insertion point in the box or until the text in the box is highlighted, and then begin typing.

Working with Option Buttons

Option buttons are the dialog box equivalent of the old multiple-choice questions you had to struggle with in school. You're given two or more choices, and you're only allowed to pick one. In the dialog box shown here, there are three option buttons at the bottom. (See Chapter 17, "A Beginner's Guide to Queries," to learn how to display this dialog box.) An option button consists of a small circle with a label beside it that tells you what the option is.

How do you activate an option button? Simply click on the option you want (you can either click on the button itself or on its name). From the keyboard, you need to press **Tab** until one of the option buttons is selected (its name is surrounded by a dotted outline), and then you use the arrow keys to pick out the one you want. As you move through the option buttons, you'll see a black dot appear inside the circle to let you know which control is currently selected.

The Add Table dialog box contains three options, only one of which can be selected at a time.

Selected   Option
option   buttons

Did you notice how the option buttons in the Add Table dialog box were surrounded by a box named View? Boxes like these are used to organize related controls into *groups*. Dialog box groups serve three functions:

☞ They divide the dialog box controls into separate areas to make it easier to find the control you want.

☞ When you're inside a group, you can select a group control simply by pressing the control's hot key (you don't have to hold down Alt).

☞ If two or more groups contain option buttons, you can select a single option button from *each* group.

Working with Check Boxes

The real world is constantly presenting us with a series of either/or choices. You're either watching Oprah or you're not; you're either eating Heavenly Hash or you're not. That kind of thing. Access handles these yes-or-no, on-or-off decisions with a control called a *check box*. The check box presents you with an option that you can either activate (check) or deactivate (uncheck).

This Toolbars dialog box contains three check boxes across the bottom (see Chapter 22, "Personalizing Access: Program Options," to learn how to display this dialog box). As you can see, a check box consists of a small square and a label that tells you what Access feature the check box controls. You know a check box is activated when you see an **X** inside the square (as in the Color Buttons and Show ToolTips check boxes), and that it's deactivated when the square is empty (as in the **Large** Buttons check box).

The Toolbars dialog box contains three check boxes that control various toolbar options.

To activate a check box, click on the box or on its name. To deactivate the box, just click on the control again.

To activate a check box from the keyboard, press **Tab** until the check box you want is highlighted, and then press the **Spacebar**. To deactivate the check box, press the **Spacebar** again.

Working with List Boxes

A *list box* is a small window that displays a list of items. A highlight bar shows the currently selected item in the list. In our Toolbars dialog box example, the Toolbars control is a list box.

To select an item from a list box, you can:

☛ Click on the item if it's visible.

OR

☛ Use the scroll bars on the right side of the list box, if necessary, to display the item and then click on it. (If you're a little leery of those scroll bar things, see the section titled "Scroll Bar School," later in this chapter.)

Here's a spiffy tip that can save you oodles of time. Once you're inside a list box, press the first letter of the item you want. Access leaps down the list and highlights the first item in the list that starts with the letter you pressed. If you keep typing, Access tries to find any item that matches the letters you've entered.

To select a list box item from your keyboard, press **Tab** until an item in the list is selected (you'll see a dotted line around the item), and then use the up and down arrow keys (or Page Up and Page Down if the list is a long one) to highlight the item you want.

Working with Drop-Down Lists

A *drop-down list*, like some weird breeding experiment gone awry, is a hybrid control that combines aspects of both text boxes and pull-down menus. You can type in the name of the item you want, or you can select the item from a list that drops down (hence the name) when you select the control. Drop-downs usually contain lists of related items, such as disk drives or object properties. The Open Database dialog box shown here has two drop-down lists: List Files of Type and Drives (see Chapter 6, "Databasics: Working with Access

Not all list boxes are created equal. Some are creatures called *combination list boxes* (they also go by the rather jaunty name *combo boxes*), because they combine a text box with a list box. This means that, besides selecting an item from the list, you can also use the text box to type in the name of the item you want. Chapter 6, "Databasics: Working with Access Databases," gives you a good example of a combination list box.

Databases," to get the full scoop on the Open Database dialog box). In this case, the Drives control has been dropped down to display the items in the list.

Drop-down list

Drop-down list that has been dropped down

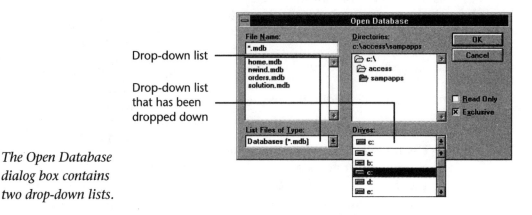

The Open Database dialog box contains two drop-down lists.

Selecting Stuff from Drop-Down List Boxes

To select an item from a drop-down list, follow these steps:

1. Click on the downward-pointing arrow on the right side of the control. This opens the list to display its options.

2. Click on the item you want. If you don't see the item you want, use the scroll bar to view more of the list. (If you're not sure how a scroll bar works, see the next section.)

To use your keyboard to select an item from a drop-down list, follow these steps:

1. Press **Tab** until the item inside the drop-down list's text box is selected.

2. Press the down arrow key to open the list. (Confusingly, some drop-down lists require you to press Alt+down arrow to display the list.)

3. Use the up and down arrow keys to highlight the item you want.

4. Press **Enter**.

Scroll Bar School

Some lists contain too many items to fit inside the box. In this case, a *scroll bar* appears on the right hand side of the box to make it easier to navigate the list. These scroll bars are a lot like elevators. They sort of look like elevator shafts, and, like your favorite Otis device, they serve a dual purpose: they can tell you where you are, and they can take you somewhere else.

As you'll see throughout this book, Access uses *lots* of drop-down lists, so a careful perusal of this material will be well worth the effort down the road.

Where Am I? The Scroll Bar Knows

Thanks to my innately lousy sense of direction, I always seem to get lost in long lists of items. Fortunately, I have scroll bars to bail me out. The idea is simple: each scroll bar contains a small box (called, appropriately enough, the *scroll box*) that tells me my relative position in the list. So, for example, if the scroll box is about halfway down, then I know I'm somewhere near the middle of the list. They're just like the floor indicators on an elevator.

Can I Get There from Here? Navigating with Scroll Bars

The real scroll bar fun begins when you use them to move around in your lists. There are three basic techniques:

- ☞ To scroll through the list one line at a time, click on the scroll bar's up or down scroll arrows.

- ☞ To leap through a long list several items at a time, click inside the scroll bar between the scroll box and the scroll arrows. For example, to move down several items, click inside the scroll bar between the scroll box and the down scroll arrow.

- ☞ To move to a specific part of the list, drag the scroll box up or down to the appropriate position. For example, to move to the beginning of a list, drag the scroll box to the top.

The Least You Need to Know

This chapter showed you the ins and outs of using dialog boxes to communicate with Access. We covered a lot of ground, and you learned all kinds of new things. If it's not all clear in your head right now, don't worry about it because, believe me, you'll be getting plenty of practice. In the meantime, here's some important stuff to remember:

☞ Access uses dialog boxes to ask you for more information or to confirm that the command you've selected is what you really want to do.

☞ Keyboard jockeys use the Tab key (or Shift+Tab) to move through the dialog box controls.

☞ Many controls have underlined letters. When you're in a group, you can select these controls by pressing the letter on your keyboard. Outside the group, you can select a control by holding down **Alt** and pressing the control's underlined letter.

☞ Most dialog boxes use the OK and Cancel buttons. Select **OK** to exit the dialog box and put your choices into effect. Select **Cancel** to bail out of a dialog box without doing anything.

Chapter 6

Databasics: Working with Access Databases

In This Chapter

☞ How to create a new Access database

☞ Getting comfortable with the database window

☞ Closing a database

☞ Opening databases that already exist

☞ Thrilling and unexpurgated coverage of basic Access database lore

Well, let's see: we've covered database theory, starting and quitting Access, using the mouse and keyboard, and working with menus, toolbars, and dialog boxes. Unfortunately, I can't think of any other topics we can cover that will let us procrastinate further. There's just no getting around it: we'll have to get down to work in this chapter. Sigh. The good news is that the work won't be too hard. I'll be showing you the ins and outs of Access databases so you'll be set up for the rest of the chapters in the book.

Access Databases Revisited

As I explained back in Chapter 2, an Access database is like an electronic toolshed that stores various objects. These objects include the tables that store the raw data; the forms you use to enter and edit the data; the queries that extract data from the tables; and the reports that tidy up your data to make it presentable for guests.

So, the final stage of your basic Access education is to take a closer look at these database toolsheds. I'll first show you how to erect your own database from the ground up. Then, we'll take a tour through the shed, and I'll also show you how to close up your database at night and reopen it in the morning. So don your hard hats and let's get to it. . . .

You can also display the New Database dialog box by pressing the **Ctrl+N** shortcut key combination.

Creating a New Database

Whenever you start Access, you're immediately confronted with the dilemma of that depressingly sparse screen. At this point, there are two paths you can take: you can create a new database from scratch, or you can open a database that already exists. Since we're just starting out, I'll show you how to roll your own database, and then you can use it to get familiar with Access database architecture.

To create a new database, begin by selecting the New Database command from the File menu. In response, Access displays a dialog box named New Database (makes sense, doesn't it?) shown here. The purpose of this dialog box is to give a name to your new creation.

 Clicking on this button in the toolbar will also display the New Database dialog box.

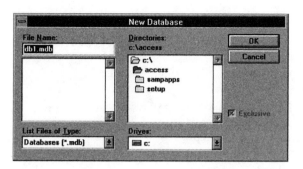

Use the New Database dialog box to name your database.

I Can Name That Database in Eight Characters

Computers are downright fussy about file names. If you make even the slightest mistake, they get all huffy and will bark some kind of error message at you. To avoid this ignominious fate in Access, you need only follow two picky rules:

☛ The name of the database can't be any longer than eight characters.

☛ You can't use a space or any of the other forbidden characters:

    + = \ | ; : , . < > ? /

When you first display the New Database dialog box, Access uses the File Name edit box to suggest a name. If this is your first database, for example, Access suggests the name DB1.MDB. Yuck! *You don't have to stand for this!* Go ahead and enter your own, more descriptive name. (Although, believe me, I realize it's hard to get creative when you only have eight letters to deal with.)

TECHNO NERD TEACHES...

What's with the .MDB at the end of the database name suggested by Access? Well, it's technically known as an *extension*, and it's used to identify the type of file you're dealing with. In this case, the MDB stands for Microsoft DataBase, and it identifies the file as an Access database. Happily, you don't need to remember to add this extension when naming your databases because Access always adds it automatically.

What should you name the database? That depends entirely on what you're going to use it for. If you're just fooling around, I'd suggest *test* or *crap* or something. If, for example, you'll be entering data on your CDs, records, and tapes, then perhaps *music* would be appropriate. Similarly, *invoices* would be a good name for a database of accounts receivable invoices. Just pick anything that will help you remember what's in the file a few months down the road. (Just so you know, I've decided to give my new database the name *idiot*.)

OOPS!

Once you've created a few database files, you need to be careful you don't try to create a new file using the name of an existing database. If you do, Access warns you and asks if you want to **replace the existing file**. If this happens, don't make any false moves, and be sure to click on the **No** button. If you select **Yes**, Access will delete the old database, and no amount of cursing or gesticulating will get it back.

Finishing Up

Once you've named the database, you can go ahead and tell Access to create it (you can ignore most of the other controls in the New Database dialog box). To do this, you just have to select the **OK** button or press **Enter**. After chugging for a few seconds, Access creates the database and then displays this window. (The name of your window may be different, depending on the name you gave your database.)

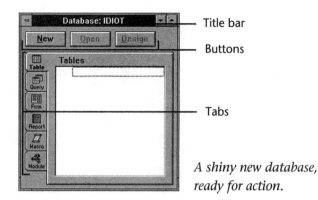

A shiny new database, ready for action.

Checking Out the Database Window

The database window gives us a view into the "toolshed" that will house the database's tables, forms, queries, and so on. Each database window is divided into the following four areas:

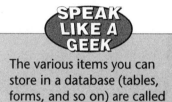

The various items you can store in a database (tables, forms, and so on) are called **objects**.

Title bar   The top line of the database window is similar to the top line of the Access window. It always contains the word **Database** (to let you know you're looking at a database and not something else), followed by a colon, and then the name of the database. I'll explain the other symbols in the title bar in Chapter 16, "Managing All Those Access Windows."

Buttons   The database window has three buttons: New, Open, and Design. You use these buttons when working with the various database objects. I'll explain them as we go along.

Tabs   The tabs running down the left side of the database window represent each of the objects you can include in a database.

Object list   When you select a tab, Access uses the object list to display all the objects associated with that tab. These lists are empty for a new database, but the picture here shows a different database that has several tables in its table object list. (Turn to either Chapter 8, "Creating A Table Using the Handy Table Wizard," or Chapter 9, "Creating a Table with Your Bare Hands," to get the lowdown on creating tables.)

Object list

A database that lists several table objects.

Access displays the table object list by default, but you can view the lists for the other object types by trying either of the following techniques:

☞ With your mouse, click on the appropriate tab.

☞ Pull down the View menu, and select the command that represents the object list you want to see. For example, to display the Report tab, you'd select Reports from the View menu.

An even easier way to close a database is to press **Ctrl+F4**. Note, however, that this shortcut assumes the database window is the only window on your screen. (As you'll see later in this book, it's not unusual to have several windows open at once. Chapter 16, "Managing All Those Access Windows," tells you everything you need to know about all this window stuff.)

Closing a Database

Although Access usually closes your database for you automatically (for example, when you exit the program, create a new database, or open an existing database), it's worthwhile knowing how to do it yourself. Besides, it's about as easy as Access gets. To close a database, you just need to select the Close Database command from the File menu. That's it!

Opening an Existing Database

As I've mentioned, Access will courteously close a database whenever you exit the program or create a new database (Access lets you display only one database at a time). If you want to return to the old database, you need to *open* it.

To open a database, first select the **Open** Database command from the File menu. You'll soon see the Open Database dialog box. The File Name list box displays the names of all your databases. To select the database you want, you can either type its name in the File Name edit box or else highlight the name in the list box. (For a refresher course in working with edit boxes and list boxes, head back to Chapter 5, "Talking to the Access Dialog Boxes.") When you're ready, select **OK**, or press **Enter**.

You can also display the Open Database dialog box by pressing **Ctrl+O**.

Clicking on this button in the toolbar will also display the Open Database dialog box.

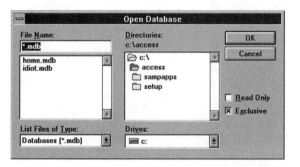

Use the Open Database dialog box to select the database you want to play with.

You may be able to open the database you need without bothering with all this dialog box rigmarole. Pull down the File menu, and look at the "commands" that appear just above the Exit command. These options all have numbers beside them, and they represent the last four databases you've worked with (there may be less than four if you haven't yet worked with four databases). If the database you want to open is listed among these four, you're in luck! Just select it from the menu (you can use the numbers as hot keys), and Access will open the database with no questions asked. You're welcome.

The Access designers thoughtfully included a sample database in your package. If you'd like to play around with it, you need to do two things:

1. In the Open Database dialog box, move to the **Directories** list, and then either double-click on the **sampapps** item, or highlight

sampapps and press **Enter**. You should see a different list of database names appear in the File Name list.

2. Move back to the File Name list, and highlight the database named **NWIND.MDB**.

When you select **OK** or press **Enter**, Access opens a database that contains all kinds of data on a fictional company called Northwinds Trading.

By the way, the next time you display the Open Database dialog box, you'll still be in the **sampapps** directory. To see your own databases, select the **access** directory.

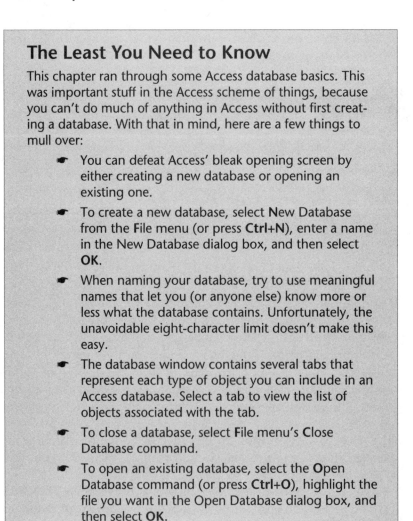

The Least You Need to Know

This chapter ran through some Access database basics. This was important stuff in the Access scheme of things, because you can't do much of anything in Access without first creating a database. With that in mind, here are a few things to mull over:

- ☞ You can defeat Access' bleak opening screen by either creating a new database or opening an existing one.

- ☞ To create a new database, select **N**ew Database from the **F**ile menu (or press **Ctrl+N**), enter a name in the New Database dialog box, and then select **OK**.

- ☞ When naming your database, try to use meaningful names that let you (or anyone else) know more or less what the database contains. Unfortunately, the unavoidable eight-character limit doesn't make this easy.

- ☞ The database window contains several tabs that represent each type of object you can include in an Access database. Select a tab to view the list of objects associated with the tab.

- ☞ To close a database, select **F**ile menu's **C**lose Database command.

- ☞ To open an existing database, select the **O**pen Database command (or press **Ctrl+O**), highlight the file you want in the Open Database dialog box, and then select **OK**.

Part II
Table Manners: Working with Access Tables

Tables are the Access database objects that hold your data. They're probably the most important objects in the Access universe because, let's face it, a database without data is like a day without sunshine. Because tables are so crucial, the seven chapters in Part II lead you carefully through the most important table tasks. You'll begin with basic stuff, such as designing a table, creating it, and entering data. Later chapters will show you how to set up your tables to suit your way of life, use forms to enter and edit info, and print your table data.

Chapter 7
The Drawing Board: Table Design Fundamentals

In This Chapter

- A brief history of tables
- Designing tables for fun and profit
- Setting a primary key
- Guaranteed painless design basics

Now that you know how to create your own Access databases, it's time to start furnishing these new buildings. Your basic decor will consist of *tables*, the Access objects that will hold your data. This chapter gets you started with tables. I'll begin with a quick description of what tables are, then go through a few simple design rules that you'll need to keep in mind when creating your own tables in the next two chapters.

Tables Explained (Again)

Although we looked at tables in Chapter 2, it's worthwhile to revisit them briefly to make sure you're up to speed on what they are and what you're supposed to do with them.

SPEAK LIKE A GEEK

In database lingo, the columns in a table are called **fields** and the rows are called **records**.

Despite their name, Access tables aren't really analogous to those big wooden things you eat on every night. Instead, the kinds of tables we'll be dealing with are rectangular arrangements of rows and columns on your screen.

The checkbook register you use to record your checks and withdrawals is a good example of a table. It has columns for the date, check number, payee, the amount of the check or withdrawal, and the balance remaining in the account. Each row represents a separate transaction.

Table examples abound in everyday life. A telephone book is a table with two fields (one for the name and address, and another for the phone number) where each row is a record that represents a particular person's name and phone number. Similarly, the contents section at the front of this book is a table (the "table of contents"). One field displays chapter titles and section headings, and the other displays page numbers. Each row is a record that tells you the page number of a specific chapter or section.

Blueprints: Table Design Questions

The tables you'll be creating for your Access databases will have this same row-and-column structure. The only tricky part is deciding what kind of structure you want to use. Fortunately, you'll find that this isn't really all that hard, provided you ask yourself three fundamental questions for each table:

☛ Does the table belong in the current database?

☛ What type of data do I want to store in the table?

☛ What fields should I use to store the data?

The next couple of sections examine these questions in more detail.

Does the Table Belong in the Current Database?

Each database you create should be set up for a specific purpose. It could be home finances, business transactions, personal assets, or whatever. In any case, once you know the purpose of the database, you can decide if the table you want to create fits in with the database theme.

For example, if the purpose of the database is to record only information related to your personal finances, then it wouldn't make sense to include a table of recipes in the same database. Similarly, it would be inappropriate to include a table of office baseball pool winners in a database of business transactions.

If you decide the table doesn't belong in the current database, all is not lost. It's a simple matter of either opening a more appropriate database or creating a new one before proceeding.

What Type of Data Should I Store in Each Table?

Once you've opened the correct database, it's time to start thinking about the information you want included in the table. For example, suppose you want to store your personal assets in a database. You have to decide whether you want all your assets in a single table, or whether it would be better to create separate tables for each type of asset. If you're only going to be entering basic information—such as the date purchased, a description of each item, and its current value—then you can probably get away with a single table. More detailed data will almost certainly require individual tables for each asset. For example, a table of CDs might include information on the record company, the number of tracks, the total running time, and so on. Clearly, such a table would not work for, say, your collection of cubic zirconia jewelry.

When you've decided on the tables you want to use, you then need to think about how much data you want to store in each table. In your CD collection, for example, would you want to include information on the producer, the release date, and the number of people the band thanks in the liner notes? This may all be crucial information, but you need to remember that the more data you store, the longer it will take you to enter each record.

What Fields Should I Use to Store the Data?

Now you're almost ready for action. The last thing you need to figure out is the specific fields to include in the database. For the most part, the fields are determined by the data itself. For example, a database of business contacts would certainly include fields for name, address, and phone number. But should you split the name into two fields, one for the first name and one for the last name? If you think you'll need to sort the table by last name, then, yes, you probably should. What about the address? You'll probably need individual fields for the city, state, and zip code.

Don't sweat the design process too much. It's easy to make changes down the road (either by adding or deleting fields), so you're never stuck with a bad design.

Here are two general rules to follow when deciding how many fields to include in your tables:

☛ Ask yourself whether you really need the data for a particular field (or if you might need it in the near future). For example, if you think your table of contact names may someday be used to create form letters, then a field to record titles (Ms., Mr., Dr., and so on) would come in handy. When in doubt, err on the side of too much data, rather than too little.

☛ Always split up your data into the smallest fields that make sense. Splitting first and last names is common practice, but creating a separate field for, say, the phone number area code is probably overkill.

Deciding Which Field to Use for a Primary Key

When you create a table, you need to decide which field to use as a *primary key*. The primary key is a field that uses a unique number or character sequence to identify each record in the table. Keys are used constantly in the real world: your Social Security Number is a key that identifies you in government records; most machines and appliances have unique serial numbers; this book (like most books) has been assigned a 10-digit ISBN (International Standard Book Number); you can see it on the back.

Why are primary keys necessary? Well, for one thing, Access creates an *index* for the primary key field. You'll be learning more about indexes in the next chapter, but it's enough to know that they make many operations perform faster. Keys also make it easy to find records in a table because the key entries are unique (things like last names or addresses can have multiple spellings, which makes them hard to find).

You can set things up so that Access sets and maintains the primary key for you, or you can do it yourself. Which one do you choose? Here are some guidelines:

- ☞ If your data contains a number or character sequence that uniquely defines each record, then you can set the key yourself. For example, invoices usually have unique numbers that are perfect for a primary key. Other fields that can serve as primary keys are employee IDs, customer account numbers, and purchase order numbers.

- ☞ If your data has no unique identifier, then let Access create a key for you. This means that Access will set up a "counter" field and assign a unique number to each record (the first record will be 1, the second 2, and so on).

Relating Tables

Access is a *relational* database system, which means that you can establish relationships between multiple tables. I talk more about this in Chapter 24, "Juggling Multiple Tables," but a brief introduction here won't hurt.

Let's use an example. Suppose you have a database that already contains three tables: Customers (which holds data on your customers, including a Customer ID field as the primary key), Products (product data, including a Product ID field as the primary key), and Employees (employee information). You now want to add to this database a table (called Orders) that will record orders placed by your customers.

When designing this database, you know you'll need basic data such as the date of the order, the quantity ordered, the purchase order number, and so on. You'll also, of course, need to record the customer placing the order. Does this mean you include the customer's name and address? No, that would be wasteful because you already have that information in your Customers table. Instead, you simply include a Customer ID field in the Orders table and tell Access that the Customer ID fields in both the Customers and Orders tables are *related*. Similarly, you could include a Product ID field in the Orders table and relate it to the Product ID field in the Product table. This picture shows an example.

This customer ID . . .

. . . relates to this customer record.

This product ID . . .

. . . relates to this product record.

Access relationships in action.

Note, however, that the Employees database has nothing in common with the Orders database (a possible exception would be if you recorded the ID of the employee who took the order). In this case, there is no relationship between these two databases.

You're Ready to Go (Finally)!

Many a huge, weighty tome has been written on the table-design process (and many an eye has glazed over reading them!). As you can imagine, most of that stuff is thick as a brick and just about as useful for our needs. This chapter's brief introduction is all you really need to know to success-fully design and create your own tables (which we'll get to in the next two chapters).

The Least You Need to Know

This chapter presented you with some basic design principles to keep in mind when creating your database tables. Here are a few highlights:

☞ A database *table* is a rectangular arrangement of rows and columns.

☞ The table columns are called *fields*, and the rows are called *records*.

☞ Your databases should be set up for a specific purpose, and the tables you add to the database should be consistent with that purpose.

☞ Decide in advance the specific data you want to store in each table. If you're not sure whether to include data in the table, add it anyway because you can always take it out later.

☞ Once you know what information you're going to store in the table, you need to decide how you're going to break up the data into fields. In general, you should break up the info into the smallest fields that make sense.

continues

continued

☛ The *primary key* is a unique field that identifies each record in the table.

☛ You can make your tables more efficient by establishing relationships between tables with common fields.

Chapter 8

Using Version 2.0's Handy Table Wizard

In This Chapter

- ☛ Starting the Table Wizard
- ☛ Selecting the fields for your table
- ☛ Setting the table's primary key
- ☛ Defining relationships between your tables
- ☛ Weird and wondrous wizardry for well-turned tables

Okay, enough of this theory stuff. It's time to get down to business and start creating tables. In this chapter, you'll learn how to command Access' Table Wizard, a handy tool that lets you create a table with only a few mouse clicks. The Table Wizard leads you through the table creation process step by step, so it's about as painless as this stuff gets. Have fun!

BY THE WAY

I'm assuming you have a database open and ready to go. If not, you should open or create one now before proceeding. If you're not sure how to do this, refer to Chapter 6, "Databasics: Working with Access Databases," to get the nitty-gritty.

Getting Table Wizard Cranked Up to Speed

Before you can start the Table Wizard, you have to tell Access that you want to create a new table. You can use either of the following two methods:

☞ Pull down the File menu, select the New command, and then select the Table command from the cascade menu that appears.

☞ In the database window, select the **Table** tab (if necessary), and then select the New button.

In either case, a dialog box named New Table appears on your screen. Select the Table **W**izards button. Access displays the Table Wizard dialog box, as shown here.

You'll be using this first Table Wizard dialog box to select fields from one of the sample tables.

About the Wizards

Since this is your first look at an Access Wizard, take a second and get to know these good fellows a bit better. As I've said, the Wizards are designed to take you through an otherwise complex procedure step by step. They present you with a series of dialog boxes that are each designed to accomplish one or two specific tasks. You just work through each dialog box, and voilà!, your mission is completed before you know it.

Each Wizard dialog box includes several buttons you can use to navigate the Wizard. This table gives you a quick summary of each button.

Click On	To
Hint	Display a Hint box that gives you more information about the current Wizard dialog box.
Cancel	Bail out of the Wizard operation without completing the task.
< Back	Return to the previous Wizard dialog box.
Next >	Move on to the next Wizard dialog box.
Finish	Complete the Wizard operation.

Selecting Fields for Your Table

The purpose of the first Table Wizard dialog box (there are, as you'll see, two or three more to slog through) is to decide which fields you want to include in your table. The Sample Tables box provides you with a list of predefined tables that come with Access. There are more than two dozen business-related tables and about 20 personal ones. (You switch between the two lists by activating either the Business or Personal option button.)

When you highlight a table in the Sample Tables list, Access displays the fields associated with the table in the Sample Fields list. The idea is to find a sample table that closely matches the table you want to create, and then add fields from the Sample Fields list to the Fields in your new table list. These are the fields that will appear in your table.

To move fields in and out of your table, use the Table Wizard buttons shown here.

BY THE WAY

If need be, you're allowed to use fields from more than one of the sample tables. Once you've added fields from one table, go ahead and select another one, and begin adding whatever fields you need.

Click On	To
>	Add the highlighted sample field to your table.
>>	Add all the sample fields to your table.
<	Remove the highlighted field from your table.
<<	Remove all the fields from your table.

When you've added all the fields you need, select the Next > button to move to the next dialog box.

The second
Table Wizard
dialog box.

Step Two: Specifying a Name and a Primary Key Field

The next Table Wizard dialog box serves two purposes. The first is to assign a name to your table. Access suggests a name, but feel free to type your own name in the edit box provided.

The second purpose of this dialog box is to assign the primary key for the table (Chapter 7, "The Drawing Board: Table Design Fundamentals," told you all about primary keys). The second Table Wizard dialog box displays two option buttons that let you determine whether Access sets the primary key for you, or you do it yourself.

Select an option, and, when you're ready to continue, select the Next > button. If you're letting Access set the key for you, you can skip the next section.

More Primary Key Fun

If you told Table Wizard that you want to set the primary key yourself, here's the third dialog box you'll see. Use the drop-down list to select the field you want to use for the primary key. Remember that the field you use for the key must contain entries that uniquely identify each record.

This dialog box also includes several option buttons that let Access know what type of data will appear in the field. You have three choices:

Consecutive numbers Microsoft Access assigns automatically to new records. If you select this option, Access will add numbers to the selected field that increment automatically whenever you add a new record.

Numbers I enter when I add new records. This option tells Access that you'll be entering your own values in the selected key field, and that these values will be numeric entries only.

Numbers and/or letters I enter when I add new records. This option also tells Access that you'll be entering your own key values, and the entries might be numbers, letters, or combinations of both.

If you don't see a field you need among any of the Sample Fields, you have two choices: if you're missing just one or two fields, you can add them yourself later on; if you're missing many fields, you may need to create the entire table from scratch. In either case, you should read Chapter 9, "Creating a Table with Your Bare Hands," to get the appropriate instructions.

Your table names can be a maximum of 64 characters long (including spaces), but they can't include exclamation marks (!), periods (.), square brackets ([ ]), or back quotes ('). Also, you can't use the name of an existing table in the same database.

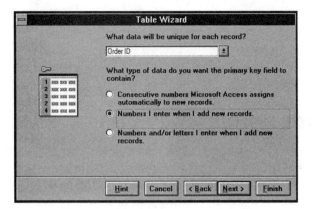

This Table Wizard dialog box appears if you decided to set the primary key field yourself.

When you're done, select Next > to move on to the next step. The dialog box that appears depends on whether you've defined other tables in the database. If you have, you'll see this Table Wizard dialog box. If you don't have any other tables, you'll see a dialog box with a checkered flag (indicating that you reached the *finish line*; how cute). In this case, you can skip down to the section titled "Finishing Up the Table."

You'll see this Table Wizard dialog box if you have other tables in your database.

Relating Your Tables

As you learned in Chapter 7, you can establish relationships between two or more tables that have at least one field in common. In the preceding dialog box, Table Wizard first tries to guess at the relationships you want:

☞ If your new table uses a field that exists in another table, Table Wizard assumes the two are related.

☞ If your new table has no fields in common with the other tables, Table Wizard assumes there is no relationship.

If the guesses made by Table Wizard are correct, select Next > to continue to the final dialog box. Otherwise, you need to follow these steps to change the relationships:

1. Highlight the relationship you want to change.

2. Select the **Change** button. Table Wizard displays the Relationships dialog box.

3. Select the option button that correctly describes the type of relationship you want to set up.

4. Select **OK** to put the change into effect.

Finishing Up the Table

The last Table Wizard dialog box gives you three choices:

☞ **Modify the table design.** Select the first option button if you want to make changes manually to the table. You'd choose this, for example, if the Table Wizard didn't include one or more fields you need. Chapter 9, "Creating a Table with Your Bare Hands," tells you how to make changes to your table design.

☞ **Enter data directly into the table.** Select the second option button if you want to start entering data right away. You read about data entry techniques in Chapter 10, "Setting the Table: Entering and Editing Table Data."

☞ **Enter data into the table using a form the Wizard creates for me.** The third option button will create a form you can use to enter data. If you select this option, you might want to check out Chapter 12, "Using Forms for Easy-As-Pie Data Entry."

To exit Table Wizard and create the table, select the Finish button.

The Least You Need to Know

This chapter showed you how to use the Table Wizard feature to create a new table. Here's a rehash of the good bits:

☞ To start Table Wizard, select New from the File menu, and then select Table from the cascade menu. (You can also select the database window's New button.) In the New Table dialog box, select the Table Wizards button.

☞ When selecting fields for your table, look for a sample table that closely matches the one you want to create. Use fields from more than one sample table, if necessary.

☞ Keep your table names less than 64 characters long, and don't use the following characters: ! . [ ] '.

☞ If you're setting the primary key yourself, make sure you use a field that will contain entries that uniquely identify each record.

Chapter 9
Creating a Table with Your Bare Hands

In This Chapter

- ☞ Creating fields
- ☞ Assigning field properties
- ☞ Saving the table
- ☞ Moving, inserting, and deleting fields
- ☞ Useful table building skills that won't give you calluses, splinters, or dirt under your fingernails

The Table Wizard covered in the last chapter makes it easy to create tables, but it's not perfect. For one thing, while it does boast an admirable collection of sample tables, the samples certainly don't cover every possibility. For another, the tables it creates aren't the most efficient structures in the world. For example, if you include a sample phone number field, Table Wizard creates a field capable of holding up to 30 characters!

To get more control over your tables, you need to build them manually. This chapter shows you how to build your own tables and then shows you how to perform basic maintenance to keep your tables in top shape.

Getting Up to Speed

Without further ado, let's get right to work. You begin by selecting New from the File menu and then selecting Table from the cascade menu that appears. Alternatively, you can select the **Table** tab in the database window and select the New button. When the New Table dialog box appears (version 2.0 only), select the New Table button. Access displays the Table design window, as shown here.

Use the Table design window to construct your table.

This is called the *design view*, and you use it to set up the fields you want to include in your table. For each field, you need to do four things:

1. Enter a name for the field.
2. Assign the field's data type.
3. Enter a description for the field.
4. Set the field's properties.

The next sections take you through each of these steps.

Entering a Name for the Field

Use the Field Name column to enter a name for the field. This is generally straightforward, but you do need to follow these rules:

- ☞ Names can be up to 64 characters long, so you have lots of room to make your names descriptive. One caveat, though: the longer your names, the fewer fields you'll see on screen when it comes time to enter data (see Chapter 10).

- ☞ You can use any combination of letters, numbers, spaces, or characters, but you can't use periods (.), exclamation marks (!), back quotes ('), or square brackets ([]).

- ☞ Each name must be unique in the table. Access won't let you duplicate field names in the same table.

After you enter the field name, press **Tab** to move to the Data Type column (a drop-down arrow will appear in the column).

Assigning a Data Type to the Field

You use the Data Type column to tell Access what kind of data will appear in the field. Click on the arrow (or press **Alt+↓**) to display the drop-down list, and select one of the following data types:

Text	A catch-all for fields that will contain a combination of letters, numbers, and symbols (such as parentheses or dashes). These fields will usually be short entries (the max is 255 characters), such as names, addresses, and phone numbers. For purely numeric fields, however, you should use either the Numeric or Currency types.
Memo	Use this type for longer alphanumeric entries. Memo field entries are usually several sentences or paragraphs long, but they can contain up to 64,000 characters(!). Fields of this type are useful for long, rambling text or random notes. In a table of customer names, for example, you could use a memo field to record the customer's favorite color, names of his spouse and kids, and so on.
Number	Use this type for fields that will contain numbers only. This is particularly true for fields you'll be using for calculations. (Note, though, that fields containing dollar amounts should use the Currency type, described under Currency.)

Date/Time	This type is for fields that will use only dates and times. You'll be happy to know that Access can handle dates beginning with the year 100 right up 9999 (you can make up your own jokes about missing appointments in the year 10000).
Currency	Use this field for dollar values.
Counter	This type creates a numeric entry that increases automatically by one whenever you add a record. Because this type of field assigns a unique number to each record, it's useful for setting up your own primary key.
Yes/No	Use this type for fields that will contain only Yes or No values. For example, in a table of your friends and acquaintances, you could have a field that tells you whether or not they bought you a birthday present last year.
OLE Object	This type creates a field that can hold data from other programs (such as a graphic image or even an entire spreadsheet). Just so you know, OLE stands for Object Linking and Embedding and is incredibly complicated. Believe me, you *don't* want to know the details.

When you've selected the data type, press **Tab** to move to the Description column.

Entering a Description

Use the Description column to enter a description for the field. You can use up to 255 characters, so there's plenty of room to pour your heart out. As you'll see in the next chapter, the Description field text appears in the status bar when you're entering data for the field.

Setting Field Properties

Your last task for each field is to set up the field's *properties*. These properties control various aspects of the field, such as its size and the format the data takes. The properties for each field are displayed in the bottom half of the design window. To change a property, you first select the field you want to work with and then use either of the following methods:

☛ With your mouse, click on the property you want to change.

☛ With your keyboard, press **F6** to place the cursor in the Field Properties pane, and then use the up and down arrow keys to select the property.

The proverbial space limitations prevent me from covering every possible property, but here's a quick look at the most common ones:

Field Size   In a Text field, this property controls the number of characters you can enter. You can choose any number between 1 and 255, although the size you enter should be just large enough to accommodate the maximum possible entry. In a phone number field, for example, you'd set the size to 13 or 14.

Format   This property controls the display of dates and numbers. For example, the Long Date format would display a date as Tuesday, August 23, 1994, but the Short Date format would display the same date as 8/23/94.

Default Value   This property sets up a suggested value that appears in the field automatically whenever you add a new record to the table. For example, suppose you have a table of names and addresses and it includes a Country field. If most of the records will be from the same country, you could add it as the default (for example, **USA** or **Canada**).

BY THE WAY

Many properties give you a choice of items in a drop-down list. Remember that you can display the list either by clicking on the downward-pointing arrow or by pressing **Alt+↓**.

In a Date/Time field, you can make today's date the default value by entering **=Date()** as the Default Value property. For the current time, enter **=Time()**. To get both the current date and time, enter **=Now()**.

Required   In most tables, you'll have some fields that are optional and some that are required. For required fields, set their Required property to **Yes**. Access will then warn you if you accidentally leave the field blank.

Indexed   Tables that are indexed on a certain field make it easier to find values in that field. If you think you'll be doing a lot of searching in a field, set its Indexed property to **Yes**. (See Chapter 14, "The Needle in a Haystack Thing: Finding and Sorting Data," to learn more about indexes.)

Setting the Primary Key

As explained in Chapter 7, "The Drawing Board: Table Design Fundamentals," every table should have a primary key. To set up a primary key, you need to do two things:

1. Create a field for entries that uniquely identify each record. If your data doesn't have such a field (such as invoice numbers or customer account codes), all is not lost. Just set up a new field (you could even name it "Primary Key") and assign it the Counter data type.

2. Place the cursor anywhere in the field row, and select the **Set Primary Key** command from the **Edit** menu. A key appears beside field name.

Click on this tool in the Table Design toolbar to set the primary key.

Saving the Table

When your table is set up the way you want, you need to save your changes for posterity. To do this, pull down the File menu, and select the **Save** command. If you haven't saved the table before, you'll see the Save As dialog box. In the Table Name text box, enter the name you want to use for the table. Table names can be up to 64 characters long, and they can't include exclamation marks (!), periods (.), square brackets ([]), or back quotes ('). When you're ready, select **OK**, or press **Enter** to save the table.

Click on this tool in the Table Design toolbar to save the table.

You can also close the table design window by pressing **Ctrl+F4**.

Returning to the Database Window

When you've finished creating your table, you can return to the database window by selecting the Close command from the File menu. Your new table will appear in the Table list in the database window.

You can also save a table by pressing **Ctrl+S**.

If you want to return to the database window without closing the table design window, you have two options:

- ☞ Pull down the Window menu, and select the database window from the list that appears at the bottom of the menu.

- ☞ Click on the **Database Window** button in the Table Design toolbar.

 The Database Window button.

Whenever you do a lot of work in the table design window, you should save your changes regularly. If you don't, a power outage or program crash could wipe out a huge chunk of your hard work. Because saving is so easy (and because I'm a bit paranoid), I save my tables every few minutes or so.

Redisplaying the Table Design Window

One of the sad truths of table creation is that, no matter how much you prepare your design in advance, you'll always need to go back at some point and make changes. This is perfectly normal and should in no way be construed as a failure on your part.

If you need to make changes to your table's design and you've already closed the design window, you can reopen it by highlighting the table name in the database window and then selecting the Design button. With the design window back on screen, you can change field names, assign a different data type to a field, or edit a field's properties. You can also move fields around and add and delete fields, as described in the next few sections.

Moving a Field

As you'll see in the next chapter, you'll normally enter the data for each record in the same order that you added the fields to the table. If the current field order isn't right for some reason, then you need to move the fields to get the correct order. The following steps show you how to move a field:

1. You first need to select the entire field you want to move by using either of the following methods:

   ☞ Click on the field selection button to the left of the Field Name column (see the picture that follows).

   OR

   ☞ Place the cursor anywhere in the field, and press **Shift+Spacebar**.

Click here to select the entire row.

Click on the field selection button to select the entire field.

2. Pull down the Edit menu, and select the Cut command. The field disappears from the table (don't worry: Access is saving the information in a special location).

When moving a field, you can also use the following shortcut keys: press **Ctrl+X** for the Cut command and **Ctrl+V** for the Paste command.

3. Select the field above which you want the moved field to appear (you can select either the entire field or simply place the cursor in one of the field's columns). In the preceding picture, for example, if I wanted the Deposit field to appear above the Withdrawal field, I'd select the Withdrawal field.

4. From the Edit menu, select the Paste command. Access reinstates the field data above the current field.

Adding New Fields

If you need to add a field or two to your table, Access gives you two methods:

☞ You can create a new field by hand.

OR

☞ You can use the Field Builder to add a field from one of Access' sample tables.

Adding a Field By Hand

Adding another field to the table is just like adding a field in your original database design. You move to the first empty row and then enter the field name, data type, description, and properties.

However, what if you want to insert the new field somewhere in the middle of the table? You could add the field at the bottom and then move it, but Access gives you a nifty way to save a step. You first select the field above which you want the new field inserted. Then just select the Edit menu's Insert Row command. Access creates a blank field above the current field.

 Click on this tool in the Table Design toolbar to insert a row for a new field.

Another way to insert a new field is to right-click on an existing field and then select the **Insert Row** command from the shortcut menu that appears.

Adding a Field with Version 2.0's Field Builder

Instead of adding a new field from scratch, you can use the Field Builder feature to add a ready-made field from one of Access' many sample tables. To start Field Builder, first select an empty row in the table design window, and then click on the **Build** button, or right-click on the **Field Name** column and select **Build** from the shortcut menu. You'll see the Field Builder dialog box, shown below.

⬛ The Build button from the Table Design toolbar.

You can use the Field Builder dialog box to insert a ready-made field into your table.

Select an appropriate table from the Sample Tables list (use the **Business** and **Personal** option buttons to change the lists), and then select the field you want from the Sample Fields list. When you're ready. Select **OK**, or press **Enter**. Access returns you to the design window and adds the new field (you'll need to add your own description).

Deleting Fields

Deleting fields is easy. Simply select the field you want to blow away, pull down the Edit menu, and then select the Delete Row command.

You can also delete a field by right-clicking on the field and then selecting the **Delete Row** command from the shortcut menu.

 Click on this tool in the Table Design toolbar to delete the current field.

The Least You Need to Know

This chapter showed you how to create tables without the help of the Table Wizard. As you've seen, working with tables this way takes a bit more effort, but you gain much more control over the final product. Let's take a fond look back at some of the chapter's more memorable moments:

- ☞ To start a new table, select the **File** menu's **New** command, and then select **Table** from the cascade menu. In the New Table dialog box that appears, select the **New Table** button.

- ☞ For each field you want to add to the table, enter the name, data type, description, and property settings.

- ☞ Use the **Edit** menu's Set Primary Key command to set the primary key field for the table.

- ☞ To save your table, select **Save** from the **File** menu, or press **Ctrl+S**.

This page suitable for doodling.

Chapter 10

Setting the Table: Entering and Editing Table Data

In This Chapter

- ☞ Checking out the datasheet window
- ☞ Adding records to the datasheet
- ☞ Data entry and editing fundamentals
- ☞ Navigating the datasheet
- ☞ How to put your Access forks on the left and knives on the right (or is that forks on the right and knives on the left? Hmmm. . . .)

A table without data is like a Christmas tree without tinsel and ornaments. Now I'm not saying that entering data into a table is as much fun as decorating a tree (and it doesn't have lots of goodies underneath it, either!), but it *is* necessary. After all, when it comes to databases, the *data* is the most important thing. This chapter shows you not only how to enter data in a table, but also how to work with the data once it's there.

Opening the Datasheet

To enter data, you need to *open* the table. You do this by highlighting the table name in the database window and then either selecting the **Open** button or pressing **Enter** (you can also just double-click on the table name). A window like this will appear:

You use this window to enter your data. (Your window may look different depending on the table you're using.)

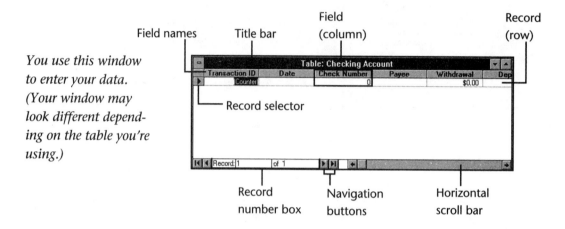

The window (or the *datasheet*, as it's called) you see on your screen may be different from mine, depending on the fields included in the table you're working with. However, it *will* have the following features:

Title bar   As usual, this is the top line of the window.

Fields   Each column in the datasheet corresponds to a field you added when you created the table.

Field Names   This is the line just below the title bar. These are the names you assigned to your fields.

Records   Each row in the datasheet corresponds to a record.

Record selector   These buttons run down the left side of the window. You use them to select records (see Chapter 11), and they also show icons that give you more information about the record (as described later in this chapter).

Record number box   This tells you which record is currently selected and the total number of records in the table. For example, **Record 3 of 32** means you're on the third record and there are 32 total records in the table.

Navigation buttons   These buttons help mouse users navigate the table. See "Navigating Table Records," later in this chapter.

Scroll bars   You can also use the window's scroll bars to navigate the table. At first, you see only the horizontal scroll bar, but after you've added a few records, the vertical scroll bar appears on the right. (See Chapter 5, "Talking to the Access Dialog Boxes," if you need to refresh your memory about scroll bars.)

Status bar   Although you can't see it in the preceding picture, the status bar displays the description for each field (if you entered one; see Chapter 9).

Adding Your First Record

When you open the datasheet, you'll see a blinking, vertical bar inside the first field. If the field already contains a value (as it might if you assigned a default value to the field), Access highlights the value.

The window you use for entering your data is called the **datasheet**.

At this point, you can go ahead and enter your data for the first field. (The exception to this is if the first field is a Counter field. In this case, press **Tab** to move to the first non-Counter field.) When you enter your first character, you'll notice three things (see the following picture):

The blinking, vertical bar inside a field is called the **insertion point**. It tells you where the next character you enter will appear.

☞ Access adds a second, blank row to the datasheet. The record selector for this row displays an asterisk. This is the *new record indicator* (see the section, "Adding More Records," to learn what this new row is all about).

☞ The record selector for the first record changes to a pencil. This tells you that you've made changes to the record.

☞ If your table includes a Counter field, Access replaces **[Counter]** with 1.

The pencil symbol appears when you've made changes to a record.

When you begin entering data, Access makes a few changes to the datasheet.

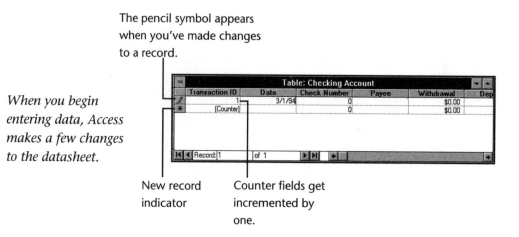

New record indicator

Counter fields get incremented by one.

You can safely ignore these distractions for now and concentrate on the task at hand. When you're done with the first field, move to the second field by pressing **Tab**, and then enter your data for that field. (With a mouse, you can also select the next field by clicking on it.) Continue in this manner until you've completed the first record.

Navigating Fields

To make it easier to enter your data, you should be familiar with the techniques for navigating the datasheet fields. With your mouse, as I've said, you can select a field just by clicking on it. If you can't see all your fields, use the horizontal scroll bar to bring them into view.

With your keyboard, use the following keys when navigating fields in the datasheet.

Press	To Move To
Tab	The next field to the right.
Shift+Tab	The previous field to the left.
Shift+Home	The first field.
Shift+End	The last field.

Entering Data

Entering data in Access is, for the most part, straightforward. You just select a field and start typing. If you make a mistake, use the **Backspace** key to delete the character to the left of the insertion point, or use the **Delete** key to delete the character to the right of the insertion point.

Here are a few notes to keep in mind while entering table data:

When you use the keys from the table to move into a field that already contains data, Access will highlight the data. If you press any key while the field is highlighted, you'll replace the *entire* entry with the keystroke. Yikes! Immediately press **Esc** to bring the text back from the dead. (See "Undoing Field and Record Changes," later in this chapter for more details.) By the way, to prevent this from happening, you can remove the highlight by clicking inside the field or by pressing **F2**.

☛ The width of a field's column has nothing to do with how much data you can enter into the field. (This is determined solely by the Field Size property you learned about in Chapter 9.) If you approach the edge of the column as you're typing, don't worry about it. Access will "scroll" the first part of the field off to the left so you can keep going.

☛ If you see a field that contains **[Counter]**, it means Access will automatically assign numbers to the field, so you can skip it. If you try to enter data in the field, Access will beep at you to let you know you're doing something silly.

☛ When entering dates, use the format **mm/dd/yy**, where **mm** is the month number (that is, 12 for December), **dd** is the day, and **yy** is the year. For example, **12/25/94** is an acceptable date. The date format that you end up with depends on the Format property you assigned to the field (see the stuff on field properties in Chapter 9).

☛ When entering times, use the format **hh:mm:ss**, where **hh** is the hour, **mm** is the minutes, and **ss** is the seconds. Military types can use the 24-hour clock (that is, 16:30:05), while the rest of us can add **am** or **pm** (that is, 4:30:05 pm). Again, the format that's displayed depends on the field's Format property.

☞ When entering a number in a Currency field, don't bother entering a dollar sign ($); Access will add it for you automatically.

☞ If you enter a value that Access wasn't expecting (for example, if you type **Maybe** in a Yes/No field), the program gets all huffy and admonishes you with the dialog box shown here. Select **OK**, or press **Enter** to return to the table and fix your blunder.

Access gets upset if you enter a value it doesn't like.

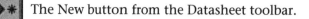

Adding More Records

You can add today's date to a field by simply pressing **Ctrl+;** (semi-colon). To add the current time, press **Ctrl+:** (colon).

Access always keeps a blank record at the bottom of the table for adding new records (it's the one with an asterisk in its record selector). The section titled "Navigating Table Records," later in this chapter, tells you how to move around between records, but for now, you can use any of the following methods to select the blank record:

☞ If you're in the last field of the record directly above the blank record, press **Tab**.

☞ Select the **Records** menu's **Go To** command, and then select New from the cascade menu.

☞ Press **Ctrl+ +** (plus sign).

☞ Click on the **New** button in the Datasheet toolbar.

The New button from the Datasheet toolbar.

TECHNO NERD TEACHES...

If you have data in a database file from another program (such as FoxPro or dBASE), you'll probably be able to convince Access to read the data into an Access table (this is called *importing* the data). Pull down the File menu, and select the Import command. Access displays the Import dialog box with a list of *data sources* (for example, other database programs). Select the source you want, and then select **OK**. In the Select File dialog box that appears, use the Directories list to select the storage location of the file, and then use the File **N**ame list to select the file itself. Select **Import** and Access imports the file into the current database, no questions asked. When you're done with the Select File dialog box, select the **Close** button.

Editing Data

Data you've added to a field is not set in stone. You're free to make changes to a field value at any time (this is called *editing* the field). You do this by first moving to the field you want to edit. If you used your keyboard, Access highlights the field value. Your next move depends on what you want to do:

☞ If you want to replace the entire field value, you can either type in the correct value (Access will automatically replace the highlighted value with your typing), or you can press **Delete** to clear the field.

☞ If you only want to change one or more characters, press **F2** to remove the highlight, use the left and right arrow keys to position the insertion point, and then use **Backspace** or **Delete**, as appropriate, to expunge the offending characters.

Navigating Table Records

Once you've added a couple of records to your table, you need to know how to navigate from one record to another. This becomes even more important once you have dozens, or even hundreds, of records in the table. Knowing how to navigate all that data can save you gobs of time and energy.

As you move through the datasheet with your keyboard, Access is in *navigation mode*. This means Access highlights each field value, and the left and right arrow keys move you to adjoining fields. If you press **F2** or click on a field, however, Access goes into *edit mode*. This means you see the insertion point inside the field, and you can make changes to the field data. Also, the left and right arrow keys move the insertion point within the field.

BY THE WAY

If you want to move to a record that contains a particular chunk of data (such as someone's name), you need to use the Find feature. See Chapter 14, "The Needle in a Haystack Thing: Finding and Sorting Data," to get the Find facts.

If you want to use your mouse for navigating, you have a couple of choices:

☞ If you can see the record you want, click on it. (You'll usually click on whatever field you want to edit.)

☞ If you can't see the record, use the vertical scroll bar on the right side of the datasheet window to bring the record into view (the vertical scroll bar only appears once you have more records than can fit inside the window). Chapter 5, "Talking to the Access Dialog Boxes," gives you the full scroll bar scoop.

Mouse users can also use the four datasheet navigation buttons at the bottom of the window. These are explained here:

Click	To Move To
⏮	The first record.
◀	The previous record.
▶	The next record.
⏭	The last record.

You can also use the **Records** menu's Go To command to navigate the table. When you select this command, a cascade menu appears with the following commands: **First** (takes you to the table's first record); **Last** (takes you to the last record); **Next** (takes you to the next record); and **Previous** (takes you to the previous record).

Finally, keyboard cowpokes can use these keys to handle all their navigation chores.

Press	To Move
Up arrow	To the previous record.
Down arrow	To the next record.
Page up	Up one screenful of records.
Page down	Down one screenful of records.
Ctrl+up arrow	To the first record.
Ctrl+down arrow	To the last record.

Undoing Field and Record Changes

If you've made changes to a record and, for one reason or another, you've really made a mess of things, help is just around the corner. Access has a couple of commands that will restore either a single field or an entire record to its original state.

If you've made changes to the current field and you want to restore the field to the value it had before you started editing, select the Edit menu's **Un**do Current Field command (or press **Esc**). Note that this command is only available while you're inside the field. If you move to another field, the command is no longer available.

If you'd prefer to restore the entire record to its original state, first move to a different field to confirm any changes you may have made to the current field. Then select the U**n**do Current Record command from the **Edit** menu (or you can press **Esc**). Again, you should note that this command is only available as long as you don't move to another record.

 Click on this button in the Datasheet toolbar to Undo your changes to the current field or record.

TECHNO NERD TEACHES...

Just as Access lets you import data from another program, you can also *export* your Access data into a different format (such as FoxPro). Select the File menu's Export command to display the Export dialog box. Select the format you want from the **D**ata Destination list, and then select **OK**. In the dialog box that appears, use the **O**bjects list to select the object you want to export, and then select **OK**. In the Export to File dialog, use the **D**irectories list to select a storage location, and use the File **N**ame list to enter a name. Select **OK** to export the data.

The Least You Need to Know

This chapter showed you the ins and outs of entering and editing data in Access tables. Here's a quick review for tomorrow's pop quiz:

☛ To open the datasheet, highlight the table in the database window, and then select the **O**pen button, or press **Enter**.

☛ To add your first record, select each field, and enter your data.

☛ To add subsequent records, select the blank record at the bottom of the table, and enter your data.

☛ If a field value is highlighted, your typing will replace the entire field. If this isn't what you want, click on the field, or press **F2** to remove the highlight.

☛ To restore the current field to its original value, select Undo Current Field from the **Edit** menu, or press **Esc**. To restore the entire record, move off the current field, and select the **Edit** menu's **U**ndo Current Record command (or press **Esc**).

Meditation Page (insert mantra here)

Chapter 11

Gaining the Upper Hand on Those Pesky Datasheets

In This Chapter

- Moving and copying fields
- Moving, copying, and deleting records
- Changing the format of the datasheet
- Printing the datasheet
- Ruthless methods for maintaining datasheet discipline

You'll be spending great gobs of your Access life entering and editing data in tables. However, most of us have better things to do all day than to wrangle with a vexatious datasheet. To that end, this chapter presents a fistful of easy ways to show those ornery datasheets who the boss is around here. You'll learn such useful techniques as how to copy data instead of re-entering it, how to adjust the sizes of your datasheet columns and rows, how to delete records, and a lot more.

Working with Fields

Let's begin with a few simple procedures that will help you work with your datasheet fields.

Selecting Field Data

The next section will show you how to copy and move field data. Before you can do that, however, you need to *select* the data you want to work with. Selecting the data means highlighting it so Access knows which data you're dealing with.

As you learned in Chapter 10, Access automatically highlights the field values if you leap through the datasheet with your keyboard. However, if you use your mouse to navigate the datasheet, or if you're in the middle of editing a field, then you can still select the field data by using any of the following techniques:

- ☞ To select some or all of the field with your mouse, position the mouse pointer to the left of the first character you want to select, and then drag the mouse over the entire selection. (Recall from Chapter 3 that *dragging* the mouse means holding down the left mouse button, moving the mouse, and then releasing the button.)

- ☞ To select the entire field with the keyboard, press **F2**.

- ☞ To select some or all of the field with your keyboard, position the insertion point to the left of the first character you want to select, hold down **Shift**, and then press the right arrow key repeatedly until all the characters you want are highlighted.

Copying or Moving Field Data

One of the things that can turn data entry into mindless drudgery is having to enter the same piece of data into multiple records. For example, if you're entering data from your music collection, you may have several records for the same artist (didn't Tiny Tim put out several albums?). Instead of typing the artist's name into each and every record, you enter it once and then make a copy. In subsequent records, you can simply run a special command, and Access will enter the copied value automatically.

Similarly, if you enter data into the wrong field or record, you can move it into the correct field. This involves *cutting* the data out of the wrong field, then *pasting* it into the correct one.

Here's how it works. First, select the field data you want to copy, as described in the preceding section. Then pull down the Edit menu, and select either the Copy command (if you're copying the data) or the Cut command (if you're moving the data). In the latter case, the data disappears from the field, but that's okay because Access knows where it is.

Now move to the field that you want to contain the copied or cut information (this is called the *destination field*), and select the Edit menu's Paste command. Like magic, the data appears instantly inside the field.

You'll probably copy or move fields constantly, so Access gives you all kinds of handy shortcuts to use. Here's a summary:

☞ Press **Ctrl+C** to copy a selected field, **Ctrl+X** to cut it, and **Ctrl+V** to paste it.

☞ Press **Ctrl+'** (apostrophe) to copy the data from the field immediately above the current field.

Access can keep track of only one copied or cut item at a time, so you need to paste your data before copying or cutting anything else.

☞ Right-click on the selected data, and then select **Copy** or **Cut** from the shortcut menu that appears. (*Right-clicking* means you place the mouse pointer over the selected data and click the right mouse button.) To paste the data, right-click on the destination field, and select **Paste** from the shortcut menu.

☞ Use the toolbar's **Copy, Cut,** and **Paste** buttons:

 The Copy button.

 The Cut button.

 The Paste button.

Working with Records

Working with individual fields is handy, but there will be times when you need to deal with entire records. The next few sections tackle the basic record techniques: selecting, copying, moving, and deleting.

Selecting a Record

As with fields, you first need to select a record before you can work with it. Access, bless its electronic heart, gives you three different methods to choose from:

- Move to any field in the record, pull down the Edit menu, and then choose the Select Record command.

- Click on the record selector to the left of the record you want (see below). You can also use this method to select multiple records: just hold down the **Shift** key as you click on each record selector.

- Move to any field in the record, and press **Shift+Spacebar**. To select multiple records, press **Shift+Spacebar**, and then press either **Shift+up arrow** or **Shift+down arrow**.

A record selected by clicking on the record selector.

Transaction ID	Date	Check Number	Payee	Withdrawal	Deposit
1	3/1/94	1	Crazy Al's Meats	$32.97	
2	3/2/94	2	Shyster & Son, Atto	$500.00	
3	3/3/94	3	Fly By Night Travel	$1,237.50	
4	3/7/94		Withdrawal	$100.00	
5	3/10/94	4	Last National Bank	$25.00	
6	3/14/94		Lottery winnings		$10.00
7	3/15/94	5	Slurp 'N Burp Resta	$32.50	
[Counter]				$0.00	$0.00

Table: Checking Account

Record: 3   of 7

Click on the record selector to, well, select the record.

With your record (or records) selected, you can then proceed with your copy, move, or deletion, as described in the next two sections.

Copying and Moving a Record

One of the secrets of computer productivity is the maxim "Don't reinvent the wheel." Specifically, if you have to enter a new record that has almost the same data as an existing record, it's much simpler to make a copy of the existing record and then make your changes to the copy.

A slightly different situation involves a record that's in the wrong position in the datasheet. In this case, you need to move the record to the correct position.

To copy or move a record, select it, and then pull down the Edit menu. If you're copying, select the Copy command; if you're moving, select the Cut command. In the latter case, Access scares the wits out of you by displaying a dialog box that says you've just deleted a record. Ignore this foolish message, and select the **OK** button, or press **Enter**.

Now move to the record *after which* you want the new record to appear. For example, if you want the new record to be record 5, move to record 4. Then pull down the **Edit** menu, and select the Paste Append command. Access inserts the copied or cut record below the current record.

Deleting a Record

To keep your tables relatively neat and tidy, you should delete any records you no longer need. To do this, first select the record or records you want to toss out. Now, pull down the Edit menu, and select the Delete command. The dialog box shown below appears to

OOPS!

As you did with fields, you might be tempted to select the **Edit** menu's **Paste** command when pasting your records. This is not a good idea, however, because selecting **Paste** tells Access to *replace* the current record with the copied or cut record. Bad news! If you do this accidentally, immediately select the **Edit** menu's **Undo Current Record** command.

tell you what you already know: that you've just deleted a record. Select **OK** to continue, or select **Cancel** to bail out of the deletion.

Just in case you have second thoughts, Access gives you a chance to cancel your deletion.

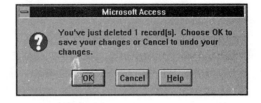

Formatting the Datasheet

The standard datasheet displayed by Access is serviceable, at best. Most people, though, have three major complaints about the default datasheet:

- ☞ Some columns are too small to show all the data in a field.
- ☞ You can't see all the fields in the datasheet window.
- ☞ The characters are a little on the small side, so they're hard to read.

The next few sections show you how to "format" the datasheet to overcome these problems.

You can also delete a selected record by pressing the **Delete** key. For even faster deletions, press **Ctrl+ -** (minus sign) to delete the current record without having to select it.

Changing the Datasheet Column Sizes

The default datasheet assigns the same width to every column. While this so-called *standard width* may be fine for some fields, for others it's either too large or too small. Fortunately, Access lets you adjust the width of individual columns to suit each field.

To change a column's width, place the cursor anywhere inside the column (it doesn't matter which record), pull down the Format menu (or the Layout menu in version 1.1), and then select the Column Width command. In the Column Width dialog box that appears, enter a number in the Column Width box. (The standard width is 18.8, but you can enter any number between 0 and 436.) If you want to change a previously modified column back to the standard width, activate the Standard Width check box. If you want the column to be as wide as the widest field value, select the Best Fit button (version 2.0 only). Otherwise, select **OK**, or press **Enter**.

You can also display the Column Width dialog box by right-clicking on the field name and selecting the **Column Width** command from the shortcut menu.

You can also use your mouse to change the width of a column. Move the mouse pointer so that it rests on the right edge of the field name box. The pointer will change into a vertical bar with two arrows protruding from its sides, as shown below. From here, you have two choices:

☞ Drag the mouse to the left to make the column width smaller, or drag it to the right to make the width larger.

☞ Double-click to size the column width to accommodate the largest field value.

Position the mouse pointer on the right edge of the field name box, and then drag it to the left or right.

Transaction ID	Date	Check Number	Payee	Withdrawal	Deposit	Cleared
1	3/1/94	1	Crazy Al's Meats	$32.97		No
2	3/2/94	2	Shyster & Son, Attorneys at Law	$500.00		No
3	3/3/94	3	Fly By Night Travel	$1,237.50		No
4	3/7/94		Withdrawal	$100.00		No
5	3/10/94	4	Last National Bank	$25.00		No
6	3/14/94		Lottery winnings		$10.00	No
7	3/15/94	5	Slurp 'N Burp Restaurant	$32.50		No
[Counter]				$0.00	$0.00	

Table: Checking Account

You can use your mouse to change the width of a column.

If you have a field with a lot of data (a Memo field, for example), it isn't always practical to expand the column width to see all the data. Instead, move to the field, and press **Shift+F2** (or right-click on the field, and select **Zoom** from the shortcut menu). Access displays the Zoom dialog box to show you more of your data. If you like, you can also use this dialog box to enter more data or edit the existing data. When you're done, select **OK** to return to the datasheet.

Another way to display the Row Height dialog box is to right-click on any record selector and choose the **Row Height** command from the shortcut menu.

Changing the Datasheet Row Heights

Another way to see more data in each field is to increase the height of each datasheet row (you can't do this for individual rows). As with column widths, you have two methods you can use:

☞ Select the Format menu's (Layout menu's in version 1.1) Row Height command. In the Row Height dialog box that appears, enter the new height in the **Row Height** text box. The standard height is 10.5, but you can try any number between 0 and 1636(!). Select **OK**, or press **Enter** when you're done.

☞ Position the mouse pointer on the bottom edge of any row selector. The pointer will change into a horizontal bar with arrows sticking out the top and bottom. Drag the mouse up to reduce the row height, and drag it down to increase row height.

Changing the Datasheet Font

The characters you enter into the datasheet all have a particular size and shape. Taken together, these properties define the *font* of the characters. Some people feel the normal datasheet font is too small and hard to read. You can remedy this by changing the font to a larger size or a darker style. To check this out, select the Format menu's Font command (in version 1.1, select Font from the Layout menu). The Font dialog box (see below) contains a number of options for changing your datasheet characters:

Font   This list is a collection of *typefaces* or character styles. The Sample box will show you what each typeface looks like, but you'll probably want to leave this option as is.

Font Style   This list contains several effects or styles you can add to the typeface. Selecting **Bold** will make the datasheet characters stand out more.

Size   This is a list of available sizes for the selected font. **10** makes the characters much easier to read and is probably your best choice.

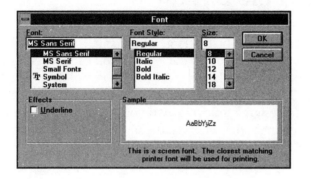

Use the Font dialog box to change the datasheet font.

When you're done, select **OK**, or press **Enter** to return to the datasheet.

Printing the Datasheet

Part V, "Data Can Be Beautiful with Access Reports," tells you all about printing out your data in the form of slick-looking reports. However, if you just need a quick-and-dirty printout, Access is only too happy to oblige.

Before starting the print operation, make sure your printer is ready for action (it's turned on, has plenty of paper, and so on). Also, if you don't want to print all the table's records, select those records you do want to print.

Now, pull down the File menu, and select the Print command. Access displays the Print dialog box. If you're printing only selected records, activate the Selection option. If you want multiple copies, enter the number in the Copies text box. When you're ready, select **OK**, or press **Enter**.

 You can also click on this button in the Datasheet toolbar to display the Print dialog box.

Changing the Table Design

During data entry, you'll often find that you need to make changes to the design of the table. A field may be too large or too small, or you may want to set up a default value for a field. Whatever it is, you can switch to the design window right from the datasheet. All you do is pull down the View menu and select the Table Design command. Access converts the datasheet window into the table design window. When you're ready to return to the datasheet, save your changes (by selecting the File menu's Save command or by pressing **Ctrl+S**), and then select the Datasheet command from the View menu.

 Click on this button in the Datasheet toolbar to switch to the design view.

 Click on this button in the Table Design toolbar to switch to the datasheet view.

Closing the Datasheet

When you've had just about enough of the datasheet, you can close it and return to the database window by selecting the File menu's Close command (you can also press **Ctrl+F4**).

The Least You Need to Know

This chapter took you through a few simple techniques to help you gain control over the datasheet. Just to help things sink in, here's a review:

- ☞ To copy a field, select it, and then choose the **Edit** menu's **C**opy command. To move a field, select it, and choose the **Edit** menu's **C**u**t** command. In both cases, move to the destination field, and then choose **Paste** from the **Edit** menu.

- ☞ To copy a record, select it, and then choose the **Edit** menu's **C**opy command. To move a record, select it, and choose the **Edit** menu's **C**u**t** command. Move to the record below which you want the new record to appear, and then choose Paste **Append** from the **Edit** menu.

- ☞ To delete a record, select it, pull down the **Edit** menu, and then select the **D**elete command.

- ☞ Use the **Format** menu's **C**olumn Width command to change the width of a column. You can also use your mouse to drag the right edge of the field name box.

- ☞ To change the datasheet row heights, use the **Row** Height command from the **Format** menu. Alternatively, drag the bottom edge of any row selector.

- ☞ To print your datasheet, select the **File** menu's **Print** command.

- ☞ To close the datasheet, select **C**lose from the **File** menu.

Okay people, move along; there's nothing to see here.

Chapter 12

Using Forms for Easy-As-Pie Data Entry

In This Chapter

- ☞ Creating fast forms with AutoForm
- ☞ Step-by-step forms with the Form Wizard
- ☞ Working with a form
- ☞ Saving a form
- ☞ Fabulously fun form finagling, forsooth

Data entry is the unglamorous side of Access. Oh sure, entering a record or two isn't so bad, but entering dozens of records quickly becomes a chore you'd do anything to avoid. "Sorry, I'd like to enter more data, but I have to wash my pit bull." The datasheet techniques presented in Chapter 11 can help, but the datasheet isn't the most attractive way to get information into a table. You can take some of the drudgery out of data entry by using *forms*. This chapter shows you how to create forms and use them to enter data. Chapter 13 will show you some nifty ways to customize a form to suit your needs.

What Is a Form?

In the real world (remember the real world?), we deal with forms of various descriptions all the time. Application forms, registration forms, license renewals, deposit slips, traffic tickets (one of my specialties, unfortunately). It's a rare day that goes by without some officious person sticking a form in our face and telling us to fill it out in triplicate.

Paper forms, then, are documents with blank boxes that you use to fill in the required information. Each box usually has a label beside it to let you know what kind of information to enter. Access *forms*, you'll be happy to know, are basically the same as their paper counterparts. As you can see in the following picture, a form is a window that displays a text box for each field in the table. Only one record is displayed at a time, which gives you two main advantages:

☞ You can see all the table fields at once (unless your table has a large number of fields). In a datasheet, you can usually see only four or five columns at a time.

☞ You're not distracted by other data in the table, so you can give your full attention to the task at hand.

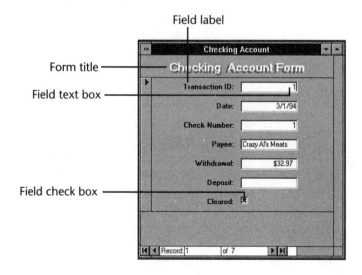

A simple form.

These advantages make data entry easier and faster. But the real beauty of forms is that you can customize them to your heart's content. This lets you create Access forms that look exactly like paper forms, and you can add fun touches, such as graphics, to make the forms more interesting. (You'll learn all about this fun customization stuff in Chapter 13, "Improving Your Form.")

Creating a Form with Version 2.0's AutoForm

By far, the easiest way to create a form is to use the AutoForm feature. AutoForm will create a basic form similar to the one shown earlier with, literally, a single click of the mouse.

The only preparation you need is to select the **Table** tab in the database window and highlight the table you want to use for the form. Then simply click on the **AutoForm** button, and in a few short seconds, your form appears displaying the first record from the table. What could be easier?

 The magical AutoForm button.

Creating a Form with the Form Wizard

AutoForm is darned handy, but there may be times when you want a little more control over the creation of your form. For example, you might want to leave out a field or two, or you might want to take advantage of the various form styles that Access offers. For these situations, you have to know how to wield another of Access' Wizards: the Form Wizard.

Starting the Form Wizard

Before starting the Form Wizard, you need to let Access know that you want to create a new form. Access, as usual, gives you a multitude of methods to choose from:

☛ Pull down the File menu, select the New command, and then select Form from the cascade menu that appears.

☛ In the database window, select the **Form** tab, and then select the New button.

☛ Click on the **New Form** button in the toolbar.

The New Form toolbar button.

No matter which method you choose, Access displays a dialog box named New Form, as shown below. Use the Select a Table/Query drop-down list to select the table you want to use with the form. (If you need a refresher course on drop-down lists, see Chapter 5, "Talking to the Access Dialog Boxes.") Then, select the Form **Wizards** button. Access displays another dialog box that asks you which Wizard you want to use.

Use the New Form dialog box to select a table and start the Form Wizard.

Selecting a Wizard

Access lets you choose from five different form styles. Each one has its own Wizard to help you create the form step by step. Here's a summary of the choices:

Single-Column   This form displays some or all of the table's fields in a column, and it shows one record at a time (the form shown earlier is a single-column form). This is the standard format and the one you'll likely choose most often.

Tabular　This form is similar to the datasheet. Each field has its own column and multiple records are displayed. I'd ignore this format altogether because you lose the benefits of the single-column format.

Graph　This form displays the table data in a graph format. This is useful for tables that contain data such as sales and expenses. See Chapter 23, "Image is Everything: Using Graphics in Tables," to get a grip on graphs.

Main/Subform　This interesting creature is actually a hybrid that combines the single-column format and a datasheet to show data from two tables at once. Unfortunately, you'll have to wait until Chapter 24, "Juggling Multiple Tables," to get the lowdown.

AutoForm　This is exactly the same as the AutoForm feature I told you about in the last section.

When you've highlighted the Wizard you want to use, select **OK**, or press **Enter**, to display the first Form Wizard dialog box. The following dialog box is for the Single-Column Form Wizard, which is the example I'll use in this chapter.

The next few sections assume you're familiar with the various Wizard controls. If not, or if you need your memory jogged a little, head back to Chapter 8, "Using Version 2.0's Handy Table Wizard," to find out what you need to know.

The first Form Wizard dialog box.

Selecting Fields for Your Form

You use the first Form Wizard dialog box to select the fields you want to include in the form. The Available fields box lists all the fields from the table you selected earlier. Use the > button to add a highlighted field to the form, or use the >> button to add all the fields. The fields you select appear in the **Field order on form** list.

When you're done, select Next > to move on to the next Form Wizard dialog box.

Use this Form Wizard dialog box to select a style for your form.

Selecting a Style for the Form

The next Form Wizard dialog box asks you to select a style for the form. You have five choices:

Standard   This style displays the title in black text and uses plain boxes for each field.

Chiseled   This style uses a 3-D box to "underline" the title and uses lines for each field that appear to be "chiseled" into the form.

Shadowed   This style creates a shadow effect under each field box.

Boxed   This style displays the fields and their labels inside boxes. The title appears as gray text on a blue background.

Embossed   This style displays the title as white text with a shadow, and the boxes for each field get a 3-D effect that makes them appear sunken into the form.

After choosing a style, select Next > to display the last Form Wizard dialog box.

Finishing the Form

To finish the form, first enter a title in the text box provided. Access suggests the name of the table, but you can change the title to whatever you want. Next, make sure the **Open the form with data in it** option button is selected. Finally, select the Finish button to create and display the form.

Navigating a Form

Once you have your form displayed, you can get right down to the business of entering and editing your data. First, though, you'll need to know how to navigate the form.

With your mouse, you can move to a field by simply clicking on the appropriate text box. (If the table has more fields than can fit on the form, you can use the scroll bars to view the other fields; see Chapter 5 to learn how scroll bars work.) To move to other records, you can use the same mouse techniques that I outlined back in Chapter 10.

If you prefer to use your keyboard to get around, here is a list of the keys to use.

Press	To Move To
Tab	The next field
Shift+Tab	The previous field
Home	The first field
End	The last field
Ctrl+Page Up	The previous record
Ctrl+Page Down	The next record
Ctrl+up arrow	The first record
Ctrl+down arrow	The last record

Adding New Records in a Form

As you learned in Chapter 10, you add a new record in a datasheet by selecting the blank record at the bottom of the datasheet. You can't see the blank record in a form, but Access still gives you a smorgasbord of methods to use when you need to add a new record:

☞ Select the Records menu's Go To command, and then select New from the cascade menu.

☞ Press **Ctrl+ +** (plus sign).

☞ Click on the **New** button in the toolbar.

   The New button.

When the new record is displayed, simply fill in the individual fields using the same techniques you learned for the datasheet (see Chapter 10). The only exception to this involves fields that use the Yes/No data type. (I explained this data type back in Chapter 9, "Creating a Table with Your Bare Hands.") These fields appear in the form as check boxes. Activating the check box is equivalent to entering "Yes" in the datasheet.

Saving a Form

You should save your form as soon as possible after creating it. (You should also save your form whenever you make changes to the layout, as described in the next chapter.) If you don't, a power failure or other unfortunate calamity may cause you to lose all your work. To save the form, pull down the File menu, and select the **Save Form** command. If this is the first time you're saving the form, Access displays the Save As dialog box. In this case, enter a name for the form in the Form Name text box, and then select **OK**, or press **Enter.**

Closing and Redisplaying a Form

When you're done with the form, you can close the window by selecting the File menu's Close command. You can also close a form by pressing **Ctrl+F4**.

Press **Ctrl+S** to save a form quickly.

To redisplay the form, select the database window's Form tab, highlight the form name, and then either press **Enter** or select the Open button. (You can also just double-click on the form name.)

The Least You Need to Know

This chapter introduced you to Access forms, and you saw how they can take at least a little of the drudgery out of data entry. I'll show you how to customize a form in the next chapter, but before moving on, let's recap today's headlines:

☛ An Access form is similar to the paper forms you get inundated with every day.

☛ To get a quick form, click on the **AutoForm** button in the toolbar.

☛ The Form Wizard gives you more control over the forms you create. To start the Form Wizard, either select New from the File menu and then select Form, or select the **Form** tab in the database window and then select the New button. In the New Form dialog box that appears, select the Form **Wizards** button.

☛ Most of your forms will use the single-column format.

continues

continued

☞ You enter and edit data in a form the same way you do in the datasheet. The only difference is that Yes/No fields use a check box.

☞ To save a form, select the File menu's **S**ave Form command (or press **Ctrl+S**).

☞ To close a form, select **C**lose from the **F**ile menu (or press **Ctrl+F4**).

Chapter 13
Improving Your Form

In This Chapter

- Displaying the form's design view
- Selecting, moving, sizing, and deleting controls
- Adding labels and fields to a form
- Working with fonts, colors, and borders
- Top-notch customization techniques guaranteed to make people warm for your form

If you enjoyed all that form fun in the last chapter, wait until you get a load of the goodies this chapter has in store. I'll be showing you how to customize your forms so they look like real-life forms, or just to give them a little extra pizzazz. You'll learn things, such as how to move fields around and change their size, how to add text to a form, and how to change colors and fonts. Let the games begin. . . .

Why Customize a Form?

Good question! Why go to all the trouble to customize a perfectly good form? The most common reason is to make the form look similar to an equivalent paper form. If the Access form resembles the paper form, the person using the form to enter data will feel more comfortable with it and be less likely to make mistakes.

For example, in the following picture, I've customized a form to look like a real check. I'd use this form to enter checks in my checking account table. It wouldn't be hard to come up with similar forms for withdrawal and deposit slips.

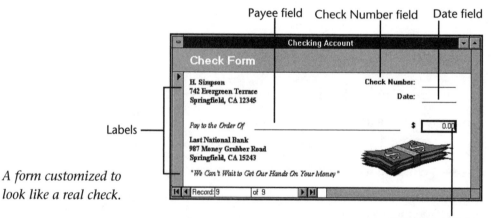

A form customized to look like a real check.

The other reason to customize forms is to make things more interesting. By adding your own text or changing a few colors, you can turn a drab form into a thing of beauty. It won't turn data entry into a party, but, hey, it can't hurt.

How much flexibility do you have in customizing your forms? Well, let's just say, I could probably write an entire book dealing only with Access' customization options. Unfortunately, we only have a chapter, so I'll just cover the basics. Here's a list of what we'll cover in the next few sections:

- Moving controls around, changing their size, and deleting them.

- Adding more fields.

- Adding your own text.

- Changing the font.

- Changing the colors.

Displaying the Design View

Access forms have a *design view* you can use for your customization chores. To display this view, try either of these methods:

Make sure you have some time to kill before tackling all this customization stuff. Once you get the hang of things (which won't take long), you may find yourself frittering away the hours playing with different options and trying to get your form just so. Just don't forget to eat.

- If you're in the database window, select the **Form** tab, highlight the form, and then select the Design button.

- If the form is open, pull down the View menu, and select the Form **Design** command.

When the form is open, you can also click on this button in the toolbar to display the design view.

When Access loads the form design view, you'll see a screen similar to the one that follows. Here's a quick look at this screen's anatomy:

Toolbar   The Form Design toolbar gives you quick access to many of the design features you'll be using most often.

Toolbox   This is a floating toolbar that contains buttons representing the objects you can place inside the form (such as labels and text boxes). If you don't see the toolbox on your screen, pull down the View menu, and select the Toolbox command.

You can also click on this button in the Form Design toolbar to display the Toolbox.

Form Header   This is the top part of the form. You can use this area to enter a title for the form.

Detail   This area takes up the bulk of the form window. It's where you place the table's fields and their labels.

Form Footer   This is the bottom part of the form. You can use this area for instructions on how to fill out the form or whatever other text suits your fancy.

The form design view, ready for action.

Working with Controls

The various objects you can place inside a form (things like labels and text boxes) are called *controls*. The next few sections look at the four most common actions you can perform with controls: selecting, moving, sizing, and deleting.

To make sure you don't lose your work if a power failure occurs, make sure you save the form regularly. To save, pull down the **File** menu, and select the **S**ave command (or press **Ctrl+S**).

Selecting Controls

Before you can do anything to a control, you have to select it. Access, as usual, has a few hundred ways to do this, but I'll only tell you about the two easiest ones:

- ☛ To select a single control, click on it.

- ☛ To select several controls, hold down the **Shift** key and click on each one.

Access places little boxes around the edges of a selected control (check out the following screen). The larger box in the upper left corner is called a *move handle*, and the other, smaller boxes are called *sizing handles*. As you've no doubt guessed by now, you use these boxes to move and size the controls. The next two sections fill you in on the gory details.

BY THE WAY

No, unfortunately, Access doesn't provide a way to select controls solely with the keyboard. The one bone thrown to keyboard types is that, once you've selected a control with the mouse, you can select different controls by pressing **Tab** (or **Shift+Tab**).

Access places boxes around the edges of a selected control.

Field controls and their labels are "attached"; if you select one, the other also sprouts a move handle. For example, if you select a field's text box, its associated label displays a move handle. I'll discuss the implications of this behavior in the next section.

Moving Controls

When you need to rearrange your form's controls, you can move them to any part of the form window. Here's the basic technique:

1. Select the control you want to move. (If need be, you can select multiple controls and move them all at once.)

2. Position the mouse pointer over the control's move handle. The mouse pointer becomes a hand with a pointing finger.

3. Press and hold down the left mouse button, and then move the mouse (this is called *dragging* the control). As you move the mouse, the outline of the control moves as well.

4. When the outline is in its new position, release the mouse button. Access moves the control to the new position.

If you're moving a field, there's a way to move both the field and its attached label at the same time. You follow the same steps as above, except you don't position the mouse pointer over the move handle. Instead, place it over the top or bottom edge of the field until the pointer changes to a hand with all five fingers displayed. This tells Access you want to move the field and its label at the same time.

Sizing Controls

One of the big problems with either AutoForm or the Form Wizard, is that they rarely seem to make form fields the proper size. They always seem to be either too big or too small. You can remedy this by sizing your fields to the dimensions you want (this works for any other control, too).

To size a control, select it, and then place the mouse pointer over one of the sizing handles. When the mouse is positioned correctly, the pointer changes to a two-headed arrow. Just drag the sizing handle in the direction you want, and Access displays an outline that shows you what the new size will be.

Which sizing handle do you use? Well, if you want to make the control longer or shorter, the sizing handle in the middle of the right side of the control is best. If you want to make the control taller or shorter, use the handle in the middle of the top or bottom borders.

Deleting Controls

Deleting controls you don't need in the form is a no-brainer. Just select the control, pull down the Edit menu, and select the Delete command. That's it! No muss, no fuss!

For even easier deleting, select the control and then press **Delete**.

Working with Labels

Labels are controls that display text. They're mostly used to identify fields, but you can also use them to add titles and subtitles to a form, or to add extra instructions. For example, beside a date field you might place a label that says something like **Enter date in MM/DD/YY format**. The next two sections tell you how to add labels and change label text.

If you delete a control accidentally, pull down the Edit menu, and select the Undo Delete command (or press **Ctrl+Z**). Undo can also reverse most other form design actions but its name varies depending on what you're trying to undo (for example, **U**ndo Move or **U**ndo Sizing).

Adding a Label

To add a label to a form, follow these steps:

1. Click on the **Label** button in the Toolbox.

    The Label button.

2. Move the mouse pointer into the form, and position it where you want the upper-left corner of the label to appear. Inside the form, the mouse pointer appears as a crosshair with a large **A** beside it.

3. Press and hold down the left mouse button, and then drag the mouse down and to the right until the label is the size and shape you want.

4. Release the mouse button. Access creates a label box with an insertion point on the right-hand side.

5. Type the text you want to appear in the label. When you're done, press **Enter**, or click on an empty part of the form.

Changing Label Text

Changing the text of an existing label is easy. Just click on the label once to select it, and then click again at the point where you want to make changes. An insertion point appears, and you can edit the text normally. When you're done, press **Enter**, or click on an empty part of the form.

BY THE WAY

Access always creates a text box when you add a field. If you'd rather use a check box for a Yes/No field, then you need to click on the **Check Box** button in the Toolbox before adding the field.

 The Check Box button.

Adding a Field

Most form design work you do involves table fields in one form or another. You already know how to move, size, and delete field controls, but what if you need to add a field you left out of the original form? Easier done than said, as this section will show.

The first thing you need to do is display the *field list*, which is, not surprisingly, a list of fields from the table you're using. You display this list by selecting the View menu's Field List command.

To add a field to a form, move the mouse pointer into the field list and place it over the field's name. Press and hold the left mouse button, then drag the field name out of the list and into the form's Detail area. (Inside the form, the mouse pointer becomes a small bar.) When you release the mouse button, Access creates both a label and a text box for the field. You'll need to change the label to something that describes the field, and you may need to change the size of both the label and text box.

 You can also display the field list by clicking on this button in the toolbar.

Working with Fonts

If you want to change the font used in a control, the Form Design toolbar gives you the following tools:

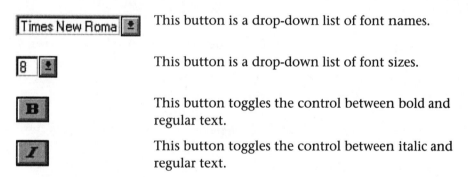

This button is a drop-down list of font names.

This button is a drop-down list of font sizes.

This button toggles the control between bold and regular text.

This button toggles the control between italic and regular text.

Working with Alignment

Alignment refers to the positioning of the text inside a control. The Form Design toolbar gives you three options:

 This button aligns the text with the left side of the control.

This button centers the text within the control.

This button aligns the text with the right side of the control.

Working with Colors and Borders

To really jazz up your form, Access offers the Palette tool that lets you set colors, try different control borders, and apply special effects. To display the Palette, select the View menu's Palette command. You'll see the Palette appear on your screen, as shown here. To apply the Palette options to a control, select the control, and then click on the appropriate Palette buttons.

 You can also display the Palette by clicking on this button in the Form Design toolbar.

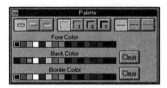

The Palette tool.

To apply colors to a control, use the three color bars shown in the Palette. Fore Color sets the foreground color (that is, the color of the contents of the control), Back Color sets the color of the control's background, and Border Color sets the color of the control's border.

The buttons along the top of the palette determine the look of the control's border. The left three buttons set the border as Normal, Raised, or Sunken. The four buttons in the middle determine the thickness of the border. The three buttons on the right set the border as Solid, Dashes, or Dots.

Closing the Design View

While you're customizing your form, you might want to see how the form looks without the design accoutrements. You can do this by selecting the View menu's Form command.

Clicking on this button in the Form Design toolbar also takes you to the form view.

When you're done customizing your form, close it by selecting Close from the File menu (or you can press **Ctrl+F4**).

The Least You Need to Know

This chapter showed you the basics of customizing a form. Here's the condensed version of what happened:

- ☞ To display the form design view, highlight the form in the database window, and select **Design**. Or if the form is already open, select the **View** menu's Form **D**esign command.

- ☞ To select a control, click on it. To select multiple controls, hold down **Shift** and click on each one.

- ☞ To move a control, select it, and drag the move handle. To size a control, select it, and drag one of the sizing handles.

- ☞ Use the **Label** button in the Toolbox to add a label. Use the **Text Box** or **Check Box** buttons to add fields.

- ☞ Use the Palette to change the colors and borders of a control. To display the Palette, pull down the **View** menu, and select the Palette command.

Here's that blank page thing again.

Part III
Basic Tools for Taming the Access Beast

With all the talk lately about the "information superhighway," the one question on everybody's mind is "What the heck are we going to do with all that information, anyway?" While Access is no superhighway (I was going to make a joke about it being an "access road," but thought better of it), it does let you play with massive amounts of data. The goal of the chapters in Part III is to help you get control over Access before it starts controlling you. You'll learn how to find records in even the largest table, how to sort your data so it makes sense, how to use filters to cut your tables down to size, and how to manage Access' ubiquitous windows.

Chapter 14
The Needle in a Haystack Thing: Finding and Sorting Data

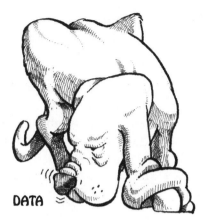

DATA

In This Chapter

- ☞ Using field data to find a record
- ☞ Finding and replacing table data
- ☞ Sorting a table based on a field
- ☞ Handy search-and-rescue techniques for finding lost data

If you've ever found yourself lamenting a long-lost record adrift in some humongous mega-table, the folks who designed Access can sympathize (probably because it has happened to *them* a time or two). In fact, they were even kind enough to build two special features into Access to help you search for missing records: Find and Sort. Find can look for a word or phrase in any field, and Sort rearranges your data in any order you choose. Sound like fun? Well, okay, but it *is* handy, so you might want to read this chapter anyway.

Finding a Record

If you need to find a record in a table that has only a relatively small number of records, it's usually easiest just to scroll through the table using your mouse or keyboard. But if you're dealing with a few dozen or even a few hundred records, don't waste your time rummaging through the whole file. Access' Find feature lets you search for a key word or phrase in any field to find what you need.

For example, suppose you have a table of invoices and you need to find invoice number 1234567. No problemo. You'd simply tell Access to look in the Invoice Number field (or whatever it's called) and find the value **1234567**. Similarly, if you want to find a customer named **Fly By Night Travel**, you'd search in the Customer Name field for, say, **fly by** or **night travel** (you only have to match part of the name, and you don't have to worry about uppercase and lowercase).

Before proceeding, make sure you have a table open in either the datasheet view or a form view.

Cranking Up the Find Command

Before you start, it's best to move into the field you want to use for the search. Although Access can find data anywhere in the table, you'll find this makes the search much faster.

When you're ready to begin, pull down the Edit menu, and select Find. The Find dialog box appears, as shown here.

 You can also click on this button in the toolbar to display the Find dialog box.

Use the Find dialog box to hunt for a record in a table.

Here's how you use the most important Find controls:

Find What   Use this text box to enter the word or phrase you want to find.

Where   The three options in this drop-down list tell Access where in the field you want to search. Any Part of

	Field looks for the search text anywhere in the field; Match Whole Field tells Access that the search text must exactly match the entire field (not just part of the field); Start of Field looks for the search text at the beginning of the field.
Search In	Select Current Field to search only in the field you selected. If you want Access to search the entire table, select All Fields.
Direction	If you suspect the record you want is below the current record, select Down. If you think the record is above the current record, select Up.
Find First	Select this button to find the first record in the table that matches your search text.
Find Next	Select this button to find the next record in the table that matches your search text. (Here, "next" depends on whether you're searching up or down.)

When you start the search, Access moves to the first record where it finds a match. If this is the record you want, select **Close**. Otherwise, you can continue searching by selecting the Find Next button. If Access can't find the search text, it lets you know when it has reached the bottom of the table (if you're searching down; see below) or the top of the table (if you're searching up). Select Yes to search the rest of the records in the table. If Access still can't find the search text, it displays a message to let you know the bad news.

The keyboard shortcut for the **Find** command is **Ctrl+F.**

When Access displays a found record, you may have to move the Find dialog box to see the data. To do this, position the mouse pointer inside the dialog box title bar, press and hold the left mouse button, and then drag the dialog box out of harm's way. See Chapter 16, "Managing All Those Access Windows," to learn more about moving windows.

*If you're searching
down, Access lets you
know when it reaches
the bottom of the
table.*

Some Notes on Searching

Searching for a record is a pretty straightforward affair, but it wouldn't be Access if there weren't five thousand other ways to confuse the heck out of us. To make things easier, here are a few plain-English notes to help you get the most out of the Find feature:

☛ For best results, don't try to match entire fields (especially text and memo fields). A word or two is usually all you really need.

☛ If you're not sure how to spell a word, just use a piece of it. Access will still find *egregious* if you search for *egre* (although it'll also find words like *regret* and *degree*).

☛ To differentiate between, say, *Bobby* (some guy) and *bobby* (as in a *bobby* pin or an English *bobby*), activate the Match Case option in the Find dialog box. This tells Access to match not only the letters, but also whatever uppercase and lowercase format you use.

☛ If you're dealing with a large table (say, a hundred or more records), you can seriously speed up your find operations by *indexing* the field you use for the search. See Chapter 9, "Creating a Table with Your Bare Hands," to learn how to index a field.

For more advanced searches, use the Access *wild-card characters*. The question mark (?) substitutes for a single character in a word. For example, searching for **Re?d** will find **Reid**, **Read**, and **Reed**. The asterisk (*) substitutes for a group of characters. So searching for ***carolina** will find **North Carolina** and **South Carolina**. The number sign (#) is similar to the question mark, except that it substitutes for a single number in a numeric field.

Finding and Replacing Data

One of the Access features you'll probably come to rely on the most is *find and replace*. With it, Access seeks out a particular bit of data and then replaces it with something else. This may not seem like a big deal for a record or two, but if you need to change a couple of dozen instances of **St.** to **Street**, it can be a real time-saver.

Happily, replacing data is quite similar to finding it. Again, you begin by selecting a field to use (as with Find, this is optional). Then, you pull down the Edit menu, and select **R**eplace, which produces the Replace dialog box, as shown here. Enter the data you want to search for in the Find What text box, and enter the replacement data in the Replace With text box. The other options are similar to those in the Find dialog box. When you're ready to go, select one of the following buttons:

Find Next	Select this button to find the next matching record without performing the replacement.
Replace	Select this button to replace the currently highlighted data, and then move on to the next match.
Replace All	Select this button to replace every instance of the search text with the replacement value. If you select this button, Access will eventually warn you that you won't be able to undo the operation. If you're sure you want to go ahead, Select **OK**.

The keyboard shortcut for the **Replace** command is **Ctrl+H**.

Use the Replace dialog box to search for and replace data in a table.

Replace in field: 'Payee'
Find What: [_____] **Find Next**
Replace With: [_____] **Replace**
Search In
● Current Field ○ All Fields   **Replace All**
□ Match Case   □ Match Whole Field   **Close**

Sorting Records

Access recognizes two kinds of sorts: *ascending* **and** *descending*. **An ascending sort arranges the data from 0 to 9 (for numbers) and A to Z (for letters). For descending, the arrangement is Z to A and 9 to 0.**

Another way to find records in a table is to *sort* the table. Sorting means to place records in alphabetical order based on the data in a field (numerical order if the field contains numeric or currency data). For example, suppose you have a table of customer names and addresses and you want to see all the ones from California. Easy: sort the table by the data in the State field and all the records with **CA** in this field will be together.

Since sorting is such a common practice, the Access version 2.0 programmers decided to do us all a favor and created the Quick Sort. This method lets you sort a table with only a couple of mouse clicks or keystrokes. To try out Quick Sort, first select the field you want to sort. Then try one of the following:

☞ Pull down the Records menu, select the Quick Sort command. Then select either Ascending or Descending from the cascade menu that appears.

☞ Click on either the **Sort Ascending** or **Sort Descending** button in the toolbar.

If you're using Access 1.1, you can only sort from within a form, and you need to use the Filter window, as explained in the next chapter.

The Sort Ascending button.

The Sort Descending button.

The Least You Need to Know

This chapter gave you the scoop on finding and sorting data in Access. Here's a summary of just a few of the amazing things you learned:

- For easier and faster searches, select the field to use for the search before starting the **Find** or **Replace** commands.

- To start the Find feature, select the **Edit** menu's Find command, or press **Ctrl+F**.

- To start the Replace feature, pull down the **Edit** menu's Replace command, or press **Ctrl+H**.

- To sort a table according to the data in a field, move to the field, select **Quick Sort** from the **Records** menu, and then select either **Ascending** or **Descending**.

**OK people, move along;
nothing to see here.**

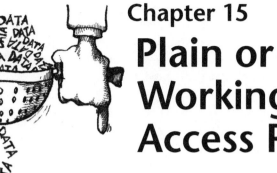

Chapter 15

Plain or Filtered? Working with Access Filters

In This Chapter

- ☛ Filters made easy
- ☛ Getting the hang of filter criteria
- ☛ Creating a filter and applying it
- ☛ Removing a filter
- ☛ How to have a good time at an Access cocktail party

In our quest to tame the Access beast, we now turn to a powerful technique called *filtering*. Filters let you view and work with a subset of your table data, which is a great way to bring a massive table down to size. This chapter explains what filters are and shows you how to create them.

What Is a Filter?

I was a corporate type in a former life, and because it's the corporate thing to do, I often found myself at cocktail parties. That's not as much fun as it sounds because, believe me, if you've been to one cocktail party you've been to them all. But the one thing I *did* find interesting at these gatherings was how easily humans can ignore a cacophony of music and voices around them and concentrate on whatever conversation they're having at the time. Our brains somehow filter out the unimportant noise and let in only what we need to hear.

This idea of screening out the unnecessary is exactly what Access filters do. We often want to work with only some of the records in a large table. The other records are just "noise" that we want to somehow tune out. For example, if you have a table of customer invoices, you might want to work with any of the following subsets of the data:

☞ Only those invoices from a particular customer.

☞ All the invoices that are overdue.

☞ Every invoice with an amount greater than $1,000.

When you filter a table, the resulting subset of records is called a **dynaset**.

A filter can do all this and more. Here's the idea: you define the *criteria* you want to use (such as the Amount field is greater than or equal to $1,000) and then, when you filter the table, Access displays only the records that meet the criteria.

For example, consider the Accounts Receivable Invoices table shown here. This is a table of invoice data for customer purchases. As you can see, the table contains over two hundred records, so there's plenty of "noise" to filter out.

Customer Name	Account #	Invoice #	Amount	Due Date	Paid?	Date Paid
Emily's Sports Palace	08-2255	117316	$1,584.20	12/8/93	No	
Refco Office Solutions	14-5741	117317	$303.65	12/9/93	Yes	12/8/93
Chimera Illusions	02-0200	117318	$3,005.14	12/10/93	Yes	12/15/93
Door Stoppers Ltd.	01-0045	117319	$78.85	12/12/93	Yes	12/12/93
Meaghan Manufacturing	12-3456	117320	$4,347.21	12/15/93	Yes	12/10/93
Brimson Furniture	10-0009	117321	$2,144.55	12/15/93	Yes	12/15/93
Katy's Paper Products	12-1212	117322	$234.69	12/16/93	Yes	12/21/93
Stephen Inc.	16-9734	117323	$157.25	12/18/93	Yes	12/17/93
Door Stoppers Ltd.	01-0045	117324	$101.01	12/22/93	Yes	12/20/93
Voyatzis Designs	14-1882	117325	$1,985.25	12/22/93	No	
Lone Wolf Software	07-4441	117326	$2,567.12	12/25/93	Yes	12/20/93
Brimson Furniture	10-0009	117327	$1,847.25	12/28/93	Yes	12/28/93
Door Stoppers Ltd.	01-0045	117328	$58.50	12/29/93	Yes	1/4/94
O'Donoghue Inc.	09-2111	117329	$1,234.56	12/30/93	Yes	1/5/94
Refco Office Solutions	14-5741	117330	$456.78	12/30/93	Yes	12/29/93
Renaud & Son	07-0025	117331	$565.77	1/4/94	Yes	1/6/94
Simpson's Ltd.	16-6658	117332	$898.54	1/4/94	Yes	1/5/94
Door Stoppers Ltd.	01-0045	117333	$1,685.74	1/7/94	No	
Chimera Illusions	02-0200	117334	$303.65	1/8/94	Yes	1/12/94
Renaud & Son	07-0025	117335	$3,005.14	1/9/94	No	

Table: Accounts Receivable Invoices

Record: 1 of 206

A table of accounts receivable invoices.

Here's another view of the same table, which I've filtered to show only a subset of records. In this case, my criteria was that the Customer Name field was equal to **Refco Office Solutions**. This shows me all the invoices for that customer.

Customer Name	Account #	Invoice #	Amount	Due Date	Paid?	Date Paid
Refco Office Solutions	14-5741	117317	$303.65	12/9/93	Yes	12/8/93
Refco Office Solutions	14-5741	117330	$456.78	12/30/93	Yes	12/29/93
Refco Office Solutions	14-5741	117343	$1,234.56	1/29/94	Yes	1/28/94
Refco Office Solutions	14-5741	117361	$854.50	3/17/94	No	
Refco Office Solutions	14-5741	117378	$3,210.98	3/31/94	No	
Refco Office Solutions	14-5741	117389	$1,642.75	4/15/94	No	
Refco Office Solutions	14-5741	117416	$422.76	5/6/94	No	
Refco Office Solutions	14-5741	117457	$879.50	6/1/94	No	

Record: 1 of 8

The same table filtered to show only one customer's invoices.

Learning About Filter Criteria

Before I show you how to set up a filter, let's take a brief look at filter criteria. As I've said, you use criteria to tell Access what subset of your data you want to see. The idea is to select a field and then enter an *expression* that defines your criteria. In plain English, filters always take the following form:

Show me all records where *field* is *expression*

Here, *field* is the name of the field you want to use and *expression* defines the criteria you want to apply to the table records. For example, suppose you select the Customer Name field and you enter **Refco Office Solutions** as the criteria expression. Then your filter becomes the following:

Show me all records where Customer Name is "Refco Office Solutions"

Similarly, suppose you want to see only those invoices where the amount is greater than $1,000. In this case, you'd select the Amount field and your expression would be >**1000** (> is the symbol for "greater than"). Here's the English equivalent for this filter:

Show me all records where Amount is greater than 1000

In the last example, we used the greater than sign (>) as part of the expression. Access has a number of these symbols (also called operators) that you can use to add tremendous flexibility to your criteria. Here is a list of the most common operators you can use in criteria expressions.

Operator	What It Means
=	Equal to
<	Less than
<=	Less than or equal to
>	Greater than
>=	Greater than or equal to
<>	Not equal to

Here are a few examples of expressions and the filters they create (I'm using the Accounts Receivable Invoices table for these examples):

Expression	Field	Displays those records where
"08-2255"	Account #	Account # is "08-2255"
<>"Renaud & Son"	Customer Name	Customer Name is not equal to "Renaud & Son"
<="G"	Customer Name	Customer Name begins with the letters A through G.
117333	Invoice #	Invoice # is 117333
<100	Amount	Amount is less than $100

Expression	Field	Displays those records where
>=1000	Amount	Amount is greater than or equal to $1,000
>#3/1/94#	Due Date	Due Date is after 3/1/94
Null	Date Paid	Date Paid field is empty

Here are some notes to keep in mind when entering your criteria expressions:

- ☞ If you want your filter to match an exact value, you usually don't have to bother with the equal to symbol (=) in your expression. As the above examples show, you can simply enter the value itself.

- ☞ Although the above examples show quotation marks around text and number signs (#) around dates, you don't have to bother with these symbols when entering your expressions. Access will kindly add them for you.

> This section only scratched the surface of this criteria stuff. For a slightly more in-depth treatment, see Chapter 17, "A Beginner's Guide to Queries."

Creating a Filter

Okay, now that you've suffered through all that criteria malarkey, it's time to get down to the business at hand. To start a filter, pull down the Records menu, and select the Edit Filter/Sort command. (If you're using Access 1.1, this command is only available for forms.) You'll see a filter window appear, similar to this one.

 You can also display the filter window by clicking on this button in the toolbar.

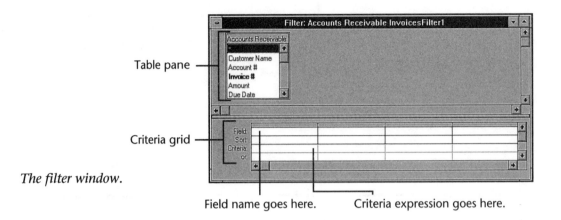

Table pane

Criteria grid

The filter window.

Field name goes here.   Criteria expression goes here.

As you can see, the filter window is divided into two sections:

Table pane   This is the top half of the window. It contains a box that lists all the fields from your table. You use this box to select which field to use with your criteria.

Criteria grid   This is the bottom half of the window. The field you select appears in the top line (labeled **Field**), and you enter your criteria in the third line (labeled **Criteria**). You can also use the Sort line to sort the filtered data.

You'll notice that the criteria grid also has a Sort line. You can use this line to sort your table. Once you've added a field, move to the Sort line, and then select either **Ascending** or **Descending** from the drop-down menu that appears.

To remind you that you're seeing a filtered subset of your data, Access displays **FLTR** in the status bar while the filter is applied.

Adding a Field to the Criteria Grid

Once you have the filter window displayed, your first task is to select the field you want to use for your filter:

☞   With your mouse, double-click on the field name in the field list.

☞ With your keyboard, first press **F6** to move to the criteria grid. Access places an insertion point in the first Field box and displays a drop-down arrow. Press **Alt+down arrow** to open the list of field names. Use the up and down arrow keys to highlight the field you want, then press **Enter**.

Entering Criteria and Applying the Filter

The next step is to enter your criteria. In the criteria grid, select the Criteria line below your field name. Mouse users can simply click inside the box; keyboardists will need to use the arrow keys. Then, simply type in the criteria. This picture shows a filter window set up to display records in the Accounts Receivable Invoices table where the Amount field is greater than or equal to 1,000.

Removing the filter only tells Access to show all the table records. Your criteria is still intact in the filter window. This means you can reapply the filter at any time.

```
┌─────────────────────────────────────────────────────────┐
│ ▭    Filter: Accounts Receivable InvoicesFilter1    ▾ ▴ │
│ ┌──────────────────────┐                             ▲  │
│ │Accounts Receivable   │                                │
│ │ *                  ▲ │                                │
│ │ Customer Name        │                                │
│ │ Account #            │                                │
│ │ Invoice #          │                                  │
│ │ Amount               │                                │
│ │ Due Date           ▼ │                             ▼  │
│ └──────────────────────┘                                │
│ ◆ ◀                                                  ▶  │
│ ┌──────────────────────────────────────────────────┐   │
│ │ Field: │Amount    │         │         │         │ ▲ │
│ │  Sort: │          │         │         │         │   │
│ │Criteria:│>=1000   │         │         │         │   │
│ │    or: │          │         │         │         │ ▼ │
│ │        ◀ ◀        │         │                     ▶ │
└─────────────────────────────────────────────────────────┘
```

A filter window set up and ready to go.

Now, all that remains is to apply the filter. First, exit the filter window by selecting the File menu's Close command (or by pressing **Ctrl+F4**). Then pull down the **Records** menu, and select the Apply Filter/Sort command. Access applies the filter criteria and displays the results.

Click on this button in the toolbar to apply the filter quickly.

Showing All the Records

When you've had enough of this filter business, you can easily remove the filter and show all the records in the table. Just pull down the Records menu, and select the Show All Records command. Access removes the filter and displays the entire table.

 You can also show all the table records by clicking on this button in the toolbar.

The Least You Need to Know

This chapter showed you how to use filters to work with subsets of your data. Time for a nostalgic look back:

- ☞ You use filters to display and work with a subset of your data.

- ☞ To create a filter, you select a field and then enter a criteria expression. This expression defines the subset of records you want to display.

- ☞ To display the filter window, select the **Records** menu's Edit **Filter**/Sort command.

- ☞ When you're ready to apply the filter, pull down the **Records** menu, and select the Apply Filter/Sort command.

- ☞ To remove the filter and show all the table's records, select the **Show All Records** command from the **Records** menu.

Chapter 16
Managing All Those Access Windows

In This Chapter

- Switching from one window to another
- Moving and sizing windows
- Arranging windows on-screen
- Hiding windows you don't need
- Rabbit taming and other risky Access skills

In this, the final installment of our "taming the Access beast" series, the beast we tame takes the form of a rabbit. Why? Because we'll be dealing with Access windows, and as you've seen by now, windows seem to multiply just about as rapidly as our furry, little friends (without being anywhere near as cute). I mean, there's the database window, the datasheet windows, the form windows, and the filter window. And we haven't even looked at queries and reports, which breed all kinds of windows on their own.

Clearly, something must be done to stem the tide. So, as a public service, I present this chapter. We'll look at a multitude of ways to manage the multitude of windows on your screen. This will include switching quickly between open windows, moving and sizing windows, arranging windows neatly, and even hiding windows temporarily.

Switching Among Multiple Windows

When you switch to a window, it becomes known as the **active window**.

Although Access lets you open only a single database at a time, you're free to open as many tables, forms, and whatever else as your computer's memory will allow. So, you'll usually have at least a couple of windows open, and it wouldn't take much to have a dozen on the go.

The first step in surviving this onslaught is to become comfortable switching from one window to another. Access gives you the following methods to do just that:

☞ If you can see any part of a window you need, click on it.

☞ Pull down the **Window** menu, and select the window you want from the list that appears at the bottom of the menu.

☞ Hold down **Ctrl** and tap **F6** repeatedly to cycle through the windows in the order you opened them. To cycle backwards through the windows, hold down both **Ctrl** and **Shift** and tap **F6**.

☞ If it's the database window you seek, click on the **Database Window** button on the toolbar:

The Database Window button.

Anatomy of a Window

To help you throughout the rest of this chapter, here's a list of the various window features we'll be using. (They're identified in the following database window.)

Title bar   You can use this area to move the window with a mouse. This area also tells you which window is the active window: it's the one that shows white letters on a dark background (inactive windows show dark letters on a white background).

Border   This is the window's frame. You use it to change the size of the window with a mouse.

Maximize button   You use this button to increase the window to its largest extent.

Minimize button   This button shrinks the window to an icon.

Control-menu box   This object contains a pull-down menu with commands to let you work with a window from your keyboard.

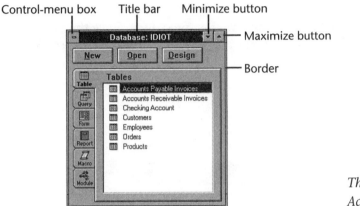

The anatomy of an Access window.

Sizing Up Your Windows

If you'd like to see more data in a window (or less, for that matter), one way to do it is to change the size of the window. This is easiest (by far) with a mouse, but the keyboard will do in a pinch.

The secret to sizing a window with the mouse is to use the *borders* that frame the window. All you do is drag the appropriate border until the window is the size you want. Which border is the "appropriate" one? Well, if you want a taller window, you can either drag the top border up or the bottom border down; if you want a wider window, drag the left border to the left or the right border to the right. As you're dragging, Access displays a gray outline to show you the new size. When things look about right, release the mouse button, and Access redraws the window in the new size.

It's possible to size two borders at the same time. Just position the mouse pointer on a window corner and then, when you drag the mouse, the two sides that create the corner will move.

Here's a refresher course on dragging the mouse, in case you forgot. First, position the pointer over the object you want to drag (a window border, in this case), and then press and hold down the left mouse button. Now, move the mouse to wherever you want to go, and then release the button.

If you prefer to use the keyboard, switch to the window you want to size and then press **Alt+ -** (hyphen). This opens the window's Control menu, as shown here. Select the **S**ize command (you'll see a gray outline appear around the window), and then use the arrow keys to size the window outline. (If you decide you don't want the window resized after all, just press **Esc**). Once the outline is the size you want, press **Enter**. Access redisplays the window in the new size.

Keyboard connoisseurs use the Control menu to work with their windows.

Control menu

	Table: Checking Account		
	Check Number	Payee	Withdrawal	Deposit
Restore	4	1 Crazy Al's Meats	$32.97	
Move	4	2 Shyster & Son, Attorneys at Law	$500.00	
Size	4	3 Fly By Night Travel	$1,237.50	
Minimize	4	Withdrawal	$100.00	
Maximize	4	4 Last National Bank	$25.00	
	4	Lottery winnings		$10.00
Close Ctrl+F4	4	5 Slurp 'N Burp Restaurant	$32.50	
Next Ctrl+F6	8		$0.00	$0.00

Windows on the Move

One of the problems with having several windows open at once is they have a nasty habit of overlapping each other. And, it never fails that what gets over- lapped in a window is precisely the information you want to see. (Chalk up another one for Murphy's Law, I guess.) Instead of cursing Access' ancestry, you can try moving your windows around so they don't overlap (or so they overlap less).

Things are, once again, *way* easier with a mouse: all you do is drag the window's title bar. As you do, Access displays a gray outline of the window. When you've got the outline where you want it, just release the mouse button, and Access redisplays the window in the new location.

If you use a keyboard, switch to the window you want to move, and press **Alt+ -** (hyphen) to open the Control menu. Select the **M**ove command (again, a gray outline appears around the window), and then use the arrow keys to move the window outline. When the outline is in the location you want, press **Enter**. Access redisplays the window in the new location.

If you change your mind about moving the window, you can press the **Esc** key at any time to bail out of the move.

Letting Access Do the Work: Cascading and Tiling

All this moving and sizing stuff is fine for people with time to kill. The rest of us just want to get the job done and move on. To that end, Access includes Cascade and Tile commands that will arrange your windows for you automatically.

The Cascade command arranges your open windows in a cool, waterfall pattern. This is good for those times when you want things nice and neat, but you don't need to see what's in the other windows. To cascade your windows, select the Cascade command from the **W**indow menu.

The Tile command divides up your screen and gives equal real estate to each window, as shown here.

The Tile command gives each of your open windows an equal amount of screen space.

This pattern lets you work in one window and still keep an eye on what's happening in the other windows (you never know what those pesky, little devils might be up to). To tile your windows, pull down the Window menu, and select the Tile command.

The Minimalist Approach: How to Minimize a Window

You'll often find you have a window or two you know you won't need for a while. You could move them out of the way or make them smaller, but that takes time, and our goal is always to make things as easy as possible. Fortunately, there's an alternative: you can *minimize* the window to a mere icon of its former self.

With a mouse, you can minimize a window in no time at all, simply by clicking on the window's **Minimize** button (the one with the downward-pointing arrow).

It takes a bit more effort if you're using the keyboard. In this case, press **Alt+ -** (hyphen), and then select the Minimize command from the **Control** menu.

Taking It to the Max: Maximizing a Window

If your goal is to see as much data as you can inside a window, then you need to *maximize* the window. This tells Access to expand the window so it fills the entire work area.

If you use a mouse, all you have to do is click on the window's **Maximize** button (the one with the upward-pointing arrow). From the keyboard, press **Alt+ - (hyphen)**, and then select the **Control** menu's Maximize command.

Restoring a Window

When you maximize or minimize a window, Access is smart enough to remember what the window used to look like. This allows you to easily restore the window to its previous size and position.

With a mouse, you have two options:

☞ If you maximized the window, the Maximize button now appears with double arrows. This is called the Restore button (makes sense, doesn't it?). Simply click on this button to revert the window to its previous state.

☞ If you minimized the window into an icon, you restore it by double-clicking on its icon.

From the keyboard, you need to do the following:

☞ For a maximized window, pull down its **Control** menu, and select the **Restore** command.

☞ For a minimized window, pull down the Window menu, and select the window from the list.

Hiding and Unhiding a Window

If you're sick of looking at a particular window, but you're not ready to close it, you can *hide* it, instead. This is also handy if you have sensitive information in a table (say, payroll data) and you don't want it displayed for the office snoops to see.

To hide a window, select it, pull down the **Window** menu, and then select the Hide command. When you're ready to work with the window again, you can unhide it by first selecting the Window menu's Unhide command. This displays the Unhide Window dialog box, as shown below. Use the Window list to highlight the window you want, and then select **OK**, or press **Enter**.

Use the Unhide Window dialog box to select the window you want to unhide.

The Least You Need to Know

This chapter gave you the lowdown on using multiple windows in Access. Here's a review of the top stories:

☞ To switch between windows, either select the one you want from the list at the bottom of the **Window** menu, or press **Ctrl+F6** to cycle through the windows in the order you opened them.

☞ A mouse is the best way to work with a window, but keyboard lovers can get into the act by using the commands found in the Control menu. To display this menu, press **Alt+ -** (hyphen).

☛ To size a window, drag one or more of its borders. You can also select **Size** from the **Control** menu and then use the arrow keys.

☛ To move a window, drag the title bar to the location you want. From the keyboard, select the **Control** menu's **Move** command, and then move it with the arrow keys.

☛ If you'd prefer Access to arrange your windows for you, select either the **C**ascade or **T**ile command from the **Window** menu.

☛ To reduce a window to its smallest size, click on the **Minimize** button, or select Minimize from the **Control** menu. To increase a window to its largest size, click on the **Maximize** button or select the **Control** menu's Maximize command.

☛ To hide an active window, pull down the **Window** menu, and select **Hide**. To unhide a window, select the **Window** menu's **Unhide** command, and select the window from the Unhide Window dialog box.

**Recycling tip:
tear this page out and photocopy it.**

Part IV
Ask and Ye Shall Receive: Querying Access Tables

Most of us don't slog through the mind-numbing chore of data entry just for the thrills. Instead, we gather our data in order to learn something about it, and when it comes to learning about data, queries are the best tools around. Queries let you ask questions of your data ("How many invoices are more than 90 days past due?" "How many Montavani records do I have?"). And the great thing is that, as long as you ask politely, Access will actually answer you! The three chapters in this section explain what queries are and show you how to create your own.

Chapter 17

A Beginner's Guide to Queries

In This Chapter

- What queries are and how they can make your life easier
- Getting started with queries
- Learning about query criteria
- Displaying a query
- A gentle introduction to a sometimes not-so-gentle subject

Okay, so you're finally getting the hang of this Access thing. You've created your own databases and tables, and you've even created a fancy-shmancy form that helped you enter data on all your company's customers. Things are looking good. Then your boss asks for a list of all the company's Swedish customers who have the first name Sven.

Quickly, your mind races through the Access techniques you already know: Find won't do the job; Sort would help a little, but there has to be a better way; Filter is close, but no cigar. No, what you really need is a *query*. You could set up the query in a few minutes and have the answer in a few seconds. It sounds like deep voodoo, I know, but as you'll see in this chapter, it's all just a matter of asking the right questions.

What Is a Query?

Queries are no great mystery, really. Although the name implies they're a sort of question, it's more useful to think of them as *requests*. In the simplest case, a query is a request to see a particular subset of your data. For example, showing only those records in a customer table where the country is "Sweden" and the first name is "Sven" would be a fairly simple query to build.

In this respect, queries are fancier versions of the filters we looked at back in Chapter 15, "Plain or Filtered: Working with Access Filters." As with filters, you select field names and set up *criteria* that define the records you want to see. However, unlike filters, queries are not simply a different view of the table data. They're a separate database object that actually *extracts* records from a table and places them in something called a *dynaset*. As you'll see later on, a dynaset is much like a datasheet, and many of the operations you can perform on a datasheet can also be performed on a dynaset.

The other major difference between a query and a filter is that you can save queries and then rerun them anytime you jolly well feel like it. Filters, on the other hand, are ephemeral: when you close the table, any filters you've defined vanish into thin air.

Query results are called *dynasets* because they're dynamic subsets of a table. Here, "dynamic" means that, if you make any changes to the original table, Access updates the query automatically (or vice versa).

Other types of queries are more sophisticated. For example, you can set up queries to summarize the data in a table, to find duplicate records, to delete records, and to move records from one database into another. Many of these more complex—but definitely useful—examples are covered in Chapter 19, "More Members of the Query Family."

Creating a Query

As I've said, the result of a query is a dynaset, which looks and acts very much like a table's datasheet. So, you might expect that the process of creating a query would be similar to that of creating a table. Well, you can move to the head of the class because, yes, they are quite similar. Both involve three steps:

1. For a table, you begin by creating a new table object. For a query, you create—you guessed it—a new query object.

2. A new table is empty, so you have to define its basic structure by adding fields. New queries are also empty and also need fields to define their structures. The difference, as you'll see, is that the query's fields come from an existing table.

3. In a table, you then need to flesh out the structure by entering data into new records. Queries, too, need records to give them substance. In this case, though, you "enter" records into the query by defining the criteria the query uses to extract records from the underlying table.

If all this isn't clear in your mind right now, not to worry. The next few sections take you carefully through each step.

Creating a New Query Object

To get your query off the ground, you can use any of the following techniques:

☞ For the table you want to use in the query, open the datasheet or form, or highlight the table name in the database window. Then pull down the File menu, select New, and then select **Query** from the cascade menu that appears. In the New Query dialog box (which only appears in version 2), select the New Query button.

 You can also display the New Query dialog box by clicking on this button in the toolbar.

☛ In the database window, select the query tab, and then select the New button. In the New Query dialog box that appears (version 2 only), select the New Query button. Access displays the Add Table dialog box, shown here. Use the Table/Query list to highlight the table you want to use, select Add, and then select Close.

If you're creating your query from the database window's query tab, you'll need to use the Add Table dialog box to select a table.

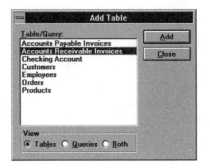

I'll talk about the Query Wizards in Chapter 19, "More Members of the Query Family."

When Access loads your query, you'll see the query design window, shown next. This window is divided into two areas: the *field list* and the *QBE grid*. The field list is, as you might expect, a list of the available fields in the table you chose. As you'll see in the next section, you use this list to add fields to the query.

The QBE grid is a collection of text boxes (they're called *cells*) where you define the query. You use the first row (**Field**) for the query's field names; you use the second row (**Sort**) for your sorting options; you use the third row (**Show**) to determine which fields appear in the query results; and you use the rest of the rows (**Criteria**, and so on) to set up your criteria.

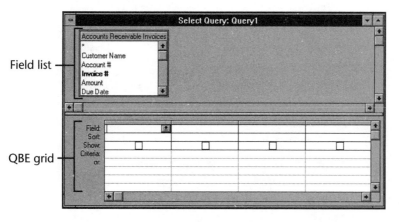

Field list

QBE grid

The query design window.

The *QBE* part of *QBE grid* stands for *query by example,* which is a method that makes it easier for us mere mortals to define a query. (The other method, Structured Query Language, is *not* something you want to know about, believe me!) The idea is that you set up your query by defining an example of what you want each dynaset record to look like. This involves (as you'll see in the next two sections) adding the fields you want to a grid and then setting up criteria for one or more of those fields.

Selecting the Fields to Include in the Query

With your new query object created, it's time to add some structure to it. As I've said, you do this by adding fields from the table associated with the query.

What fields do you add to the query? To answer that question, you need to ask yourself two others:

Double-click on the field list's title bar to select all the fields in the list.

What fields do I want to use for the criteria?   These are the fields that determine which records you see when you run the query. For example, suppose you have a table of compact discs with an Artist field and you want your query to show only those CDs from a particular group. Then you'd definitely need to include the Artist field in the query.

What fields do I want to see in the dynaset?   When you look at the results of the query, you'll usually want to see more than just the fields you used for the criteria. In the compact discs example, you might also want to see the name of the disc, the year it came out, and so on. So you'll include in the query each field you want to see.

Once you decide which fields you want to use in the query, you're ready to go. Access starts you off inside the first cell of the QBE grid, so let's see how you add fields from there:

☞ With your mouse, click on the drop-down arrow to display a list of fields from the table. Click on the field you want to use.

☞ With the keyboard, press **Alt+down arrow** to display the field list, use the up and down arrow keys to highlight a field, and then press **Enter**.

You then repeat either procedure in the other Field cells until you've entered all the fields you need.

You can also use your mouse to enter fields from the field list. There are two basic techniques:

When selecting fields, keep in mind that the order in which you select your fields is the order they'll appear in the query results.

☞ To add a single field, either double-click on it in the field list, or drag the name from the field list to the appropriate Field cell in the QBE grid. (For now, you can ignore the asterisk (*) that appears at the top of the field list.)

☛ To add multiple fields, hold down **Ctrl**, click on each
field you want, and then drag any one of the highlighted
fields into a Field cell in the QBE grid. Access enters each
field in its own cell.

Determining the Sort Order

If you want the query records sorted on a particular field, select the Sort
cell below the field name, and then from the drop-down list, select either
Ascending or **Descending**.

Excluding a Field from the Query Results

You'll often add fields to the QBE grid for criteria purposes only and you
don't want the field to appear in the dynaset. You can exclude any field
from the dynaset by deactivating the appropriate check box in the field's
Show cell. For example, the following picture shows a query with the Paid?
field excluded.

Turn off a field's Show check box to
exclude the field from the query results.

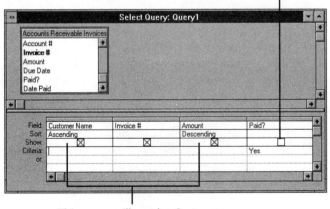

*A QBE grid with four
fields, two of which
are used for sorting
and one of which will
be excluded from the
dynaset.*

This query will sort by Customer
Name and then by Amount.

You can use the QBE grid to sort on multiple fields. For example, suppose your query will contain information on accounts receivable invoices. You'd like the records sorted by customer name, and then for each customer, by the invoice amount. Make sure the customer name field is to the left of the amount field in the QBE grid, and then select a sort order for both fields. Because the customer name field is first, Access sorts all the records by name. Then, keeping the names together, it sorts by amount.

Entering the Query Criteria

The final step in defining your query is to enter the criteria. Type your expressions directly into the Criteria cells in the QBE grid, and be sure to press **Enter** when you're done. You can use the same simple criteria I outlined for filters back in Chapter 15, or you can check out Chapter 18, "Query Criteria for Curmudgeons," to get info on more useful criteria.

Running the Query

When you have your query set up the way you want, you can run it (that is, display the dynaset) simply by pulling down the **Query** menu and selecting the **Run** command. This next picture displays the results of the query shown earlier.

You can also run the query by clicking on this button in the toolbar.

The dynaset produced by the query shown earlier.

Customer Name	Invoice #	Amount
Brimson Furniture	117321	$2,144.55
Brimson Furniture	117327	$1,847.25
Chimera Illusions	117318	$3,005.14
Chimera Illusions	117334	$303.65
Door Stoppers Ltd.	117324	$101.01
Door Stoppers Ltd.	117319	$78.85
Door Stoppers Ltd.	117328	$58.50
Katy's Paper Products	117322	$234.69
Lone Wolf Software	117326	$2,567.12
Meaghan Manufacturing	117320	$4,347.21
O'Donoghue Inc.	117329	$1,234.56
Refco Office Solutions	117343	$1,234.56
Refco Office Solutions	117330	$456.78
Refco Office Solutions	117317	$303.65
Renaud & Son	117331	$565.77
Simpson's Ltd.	117332	$898.54
Stephen Inc.	117323	$157.25

Record: 1 of 17

As you can see, the dynaset is really just a datasheet. You navigate and format it the same way (as explained in Chapters 10 and 11), and you can even edit the records and add new ones. (Any changes you make are automatically applied to the underlying table, just as changes to the underlying table are applied to the dynaset.)

To return to the query design window, select the View menu's Query Design command.

 Clicking on this button in the toolbar will also return you to the query design window.

Saving a Query

As with any other database object, you need to save your query work regularly. Pull down the File menu, and select one of the following commands: if you're in the query design window, select Save; if you're viewing the dynaset, select Save Query. If you're saving the query for the first time, you'll see the Save As dialog box appear. Use the Query Name text box to enter a name for the query, and then select **OK**, or press **Enter**.

As usual, the shortcut key for saving is **Ctrl+S**.

 If you're in the query design window, you can click on this button in the toolbar to save the query.

The Least You Need to Know

This chapter introduced you to the brave, new world of queries. Here's a retrospective look at what the heck happened:

☛ Queries are requests from you to Access to extract information from a table.

☛ Query results are stored in *dynasets*, which are very similar to datasheets.

continues

continued

☛ To create a query object, pull down the **File** menu, select New, and then select **Query**. In the New Query dialog box, select the **New Query** button.

☛ In the query design window, enter the fields you need either directly in the Field cells of the QBE grid, or by using the field list. For each field, you can also enter a sort option and exclude the field from the dynaset.

☛ In the Criteria cells, enter the criteria you want to use to define the records that appear in the dynaset.

☛ To see the query results, select the **Query** menu's **Run** command.

Chapter 18
Query Criteria for Curmudgeons

In This Chapter

- ☛ Criteria revisited
- ☛ Working with criteria operators and values
- ☛ Checking out simple criteria
- ☛ Trying multiple criteria on for size
- ☛ Examples galore to help you knock some sense into all this criteria cruelty

How many times has this happened to you: you've just finished a fun game of baseball (volleyball, touch football, hide-and-seek, whatever) and you and your pals are back at the local watering hole quenching your thirsts. Invariably, of course, the conversation turns to queries. After much discussion, everyone agrees that queries wouldn't be so bad if they could just get a handle on that criteria stuff. . . .

Okay, so it's never happened. The point is that if it did happen, everyone probably *would* agree that you can't get the most out of queries until you know a thing or two about criteria. And that's just what this chapter is designed to do. We'll look at criteria from the ground up, starting with simple criteria and working our way up to slightly more complex examples that will allow you to extract just about anything you need from any table. Is this stuff hard? No way, José! If you can dial a phone, you can handle any of this.

Criteria Redux

I discussed criteria briefly in Chapter 15, but a quick rehash here will probably do us some good. Simply put, you use criteria in a query to define the data you want to work with. In a select query, for example, the criteria define which subset of the table data will be extracted into the query results.

Query criteria operate much like the criteria we use in the real world. If you're hiring a new employee, for example, you set certain criteria for potential applicants: a minimum education level, relevant job experience, two opposable thumbs, and so on. By imposing conditions on the application process, you narrow down the number of people applying to a (hopefully) manageable multitude.

Similarly, the criteria in your queries work by imposing conditions on the data. For example, you can display records where the State field is "CA," where an Amount field is greater than 1,000, or where a Date field is between April 1, 1994 and June 30, 1994. In each case, you select the field's Criteria cell in the QBE grid and enter an *expression* that tells Access the exact condition you want to impose on the data. Here are the three expressions you'd use for the above examples:

"CA"

>1000

Between #4/1/94# And #6/30/94#

The rest of this chapter tells you how to enter these kinds of expressions (and many more) in your queries.

Understanding Criteria Operators

Most criteria expressions involve one or more values (which could be text, numbers, dates, and so on) and one or more *operators*. Most operators define a range of values for the criteria, and it's this range that determines which records appear in the query. The next few sections take you through the most common Access operators.

The Comparison Operators

The simplest way to define a criteria condition is to compare the values in a field with a predefined value. For example, you might want to see orders placed after a certain date or invoices greater than or equal to a certain amount. For these situations, the *comparison operators* are perfect. Here are all six.

Operator	*What It Means*
=	Equal to
<	Less than
<=	Less than or equal to
>	Greater than
>=	Greater than or equal to
<>	Not equal to

Here are a few example expressions that use comparison operators:

Expression	**Displays Those Records Where the Field Value**
"CA"	Is "CA"
<>"Simpson"	Is not equal to "Simpson"
<="M"	Begins with the letters A through M
123456	Is 123456
<50	Is less than 50
>=1000	Is greater than or equal to 1000
>#6/30/94#	Is after 6/30/94

BY THE WAY

Although the comparison operators list includes the equal to (=) operator, you rarely have to use it. In most cases, you can simply enter a value in a Criteria cell, and Access assumes you mean equal to (see the examples).

The Between...And Operator

If you need to select records where a field value lies between two other values, then the Between...And operator is right up your alley. For example, suppose you want to see all the invoices where the invoice number is between (and includes) 123000 and 124000. Easy money. Here's the expression you'd enter in the invoice number field's Criteria cell:

> **Between 123000 And 124000**

You can use this operator for numbers, dates, and even text.

The In Operator

Quite often, the values you want can't be described by a nice, neat range. For example, if you want to select only those customers where the State field is "CA," "NY," or "TX," there's no way to create a range that will include just those three abbreviations. Instead, you need to use the handy In operator. In lets you create a list of possible values, and then the query only selects those records where the field value is one of the items in the list. In the above example, you'd enter the following expression in the State field's Criteria cell:

> **In("CA", "NY", "TX")**

The Is Null Operator

What do you do if you want to select records where a certain field is empty? For example, an invoice table might have a Date Paid field where, if this field is empty, it means the invoice hasn't been paid yet. For these challenges, Access provides the Is Null operator. Entering this operator by itself in a field's Criteria cell will select only those records where the field is empty.

Wild Cards and the Like Operator

If you need to allow for multiple spellings in a text field, or if you're not sure how to spell a word you want to use, the *wild-card characters* can help. There are two wild cards: the question mark (**?**) substitutes for a single character, and the asterisk (*****) substitutes for a group of characters. You use them in combination with the Like operator, as the following examples show:

Expression	Displays Those Records Where the Field Value
Like "Re?d"	Is "Reid," "Read," "Reed," and so on
Like "M?"	Is "MA," "MD," "ME," and so on
Like "R*"	Begins with "R"
Like "*office*"	Contains the word "office"
Like "6/*/94"	Is any date in June, 1994

The Not Operator

Like the by now over-used expression from "Wayne's World," you use the Not operator to negate an expression. For example, suppose you want to select records where the State field is anything but "CA," "NY," or "TX." You *could* enter the other 47 state abbreviations into an In operator's list, but that sounds like way too much work. Here's an easier way to do get the job done:

Not In("CA", "NY", "TX")

Entering Criteria Values

As you've seen, expressions combine both operators and values to define the criteria. While entering values in these expressions is generally straightforward, Access has a few quirks that can throw you off at first. To get you prepared for anything Access sends your way, here are a few notes about entering values in criteria expressions:

☛ As the examples in this chapter have shown, text values are surrounded by quotation marks, and date values are surrounded by number signs. The good news is that you don't—I repeat, you *don't*—have to enter these symbols. Access is pretty smart, and it knows when you're working with a text or date field. When you finish typing in your expression and press **Enter**, Access will gladly add these symbols for you automatically. So why go through all that extra typing?

☛ When entering text values, it doesn't matter whether you use uppercase or lowercase letters. To Access, "CA" is the same as "ca."

☛ When entering values for a numeric or currency field, don't include extra symbols such as a comma (for the thousands separator) or a dollar sign. Access likes to see numbers only (a decimal point is okay, though).

☛ When entering dates, you can use any valid Access date format. For example, if you want to select records where the Date field is after June 30, 1994, you could use any of the following expressions:

>6/30/94

>30-6-1994

>30 June 1994

>Jun 30 94

Entering Simple Criteria

The easiest criteria to work with are the so-called *simple criteria*. Simple criteria are expressions that use only a single field, and so use only a single cell in the QBE grid. (This is in contrast to *multiple criteria* that use either multiple fields or multiple instances of the same field. I'll talk about multiple criteria later in this chapter.)

If you need to make changes to a query, make sure you delete any existing criteria expressions before creating a new one. Otherwise, you may end up with multiple criteria, and the results may not be what you expected.

For example, suppose you had a table of customer information and you wanted to see those customers with the word "office" in their name. You'd add the customer name field to the QBE grid, select the Criteria cell for this field, and enter the following expression:

Like "*office*"

Entering Multiple Criteria

For many criteria, a single expression just doesn't cut the mustard. For example, you know you can select all the customer names that start with "R" by entering the following expression:

Like "R*"

That's fine, but what if you also want to select customers with names that begin with "S." Or what if you want to narrow things down to those customer names that begin with "R" and whose address is in Rhode Island? Ah, that's a different kettle of fish. For queries like these, you need to set up *multiple criteria* where you enter either multiple expressions for the same field or multiple expressions for different fields. The next two sections cover the two basic types of multiple criteria: "And" criteria and "Or" criteria.

Entering "And" Criteria

You use "And" criteria when you want to select records that satisfy two different expressions. (Actually, you can use more than two expressions, but I'll keep things simple.) So, given *expression1* and *expression2*, a record only appears in the results if it satisfies both *expression1* and *expression2* (which is why they're called "And" criteria).

Let's look at an example. Suppose you want to display all customers with a name that begins with "R" (Like "R*") *and* includes the word "office" (Like "*office*"). Because both expressions deal with the same field, you simply insert the And operator between them, like so:

Like "R*" And Like "*office*"

The following picture shows these combined expressions entered into the QBE grid.

Using "And" criteria for the same field.

A slightly different approach uses two separate fields. For example, suppose you want all invoices where the customer name begins with "R" (Like "R*") *and* the invoice amount is over $1,000 (>1000). Since we're now dealing with two different fields, we can't use the And operator. Instead, you enter the expressions into their appropriate Criteria cells *on the same line* in the QBE grid. The picture below shows you how it's done.

To use "And" criteria for different fields, enter the expressions on the same line in the QBE grid.

Entering "Or" Criteria

With "Or" criteria, you want to display records that satisfy one expression *or* another. If it satisfies either expression (or both), it appears in the query results; if it satisfies neither expression, it's left out of the results. (Again, you're allowed to use more than two expressions, if need be. No matter how many you use, a record only appears in the query results if it satisfies at least *one* of the expressions.)

Again, an example will help clarify things. Suppose you want to display invoices for customers whose names begin with either "R" (Like "R*") or "S" (Like "S*"). The same field is used for both expressions, so we can simply throw in the Or operator, like this:

Like "R*" Or Like "S*"

The picture below shows this new expression entered into the QBE grid.

Field:	Customer Name	Invoice #	Amount	Paid?
Sort:	Ascending		Descending	
Show:	☒	☒	☒	☐
Criteria:	Like "R*" Or Like "S*"			
or:				

Using "Or" criteria for the same field.

Finally, as you might expect, you can also use "Or" criteria with expressions in different fields. In this case, you need to enter the expressions *on separate* lines in the QBE grid (that's why the "or" appears under "Criteria" in the query design window). For example, the picture below shows a query set up to display invoices that are either over $1,000 (>1000) *or* have a due date prior to March 1, 1994 (<#3/1/94#).

Field:	Invoice #	Amount	Paid?	Due Date
Sort:		Descending		
Show:	☒	☒	☐	☒
Criteria:		>1000		
or:				<#3/1/94#

To use "Or" criteria for different fields, enter the expressions on separate lines in the QBE grid.

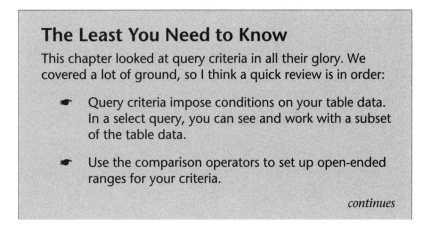

The Least You Need to Know

This chapter looked at query criteria in all their glory. We covered a lot of ground, so I think a quick review is in order:

- ☞ Query criteria impose conditions on your table data. In a select query, you can see and work with a subset of the table data.

- ☞ Use the comparison operators to set up open-ended ranges for your criteria.

continues

continued

☞ Use the Between...And operator to define a range of values for the criteria.

☞ The In operator sets up a list of possible values.

☞ Combine the Like operator with the **?** and ***** wild cards to define criteria patterns. The **?** substitutes for a single character and the ***** substitutes for multiple characters.

☞ Simple criteria use a single expression in a single field.

☞ Multiple criteria use multiple expressions either in the same field or over different fields. Use **And** criteria when you want records that match all the expressions, and use **Or** criteria when you want records that match one expression or another.

Chapter 19
More Members of the Query Family

In This Chapter

- ☛ Using a query to update table data
- ☛ Using a query to delete table records
- ☛ Using a query to make a new table from an existing one
- ☛ How to wield the Query Wizards to create other kinds of queries
- ☛ Query family values

The last two chapters got you up to speed with this query rigmarole by showing you how to work with select queries. However, you'll be happy (or dismayed) to know that Access has more types of queries than you can shake a stick at. Some of these queries are close relatives of the select query, while others are, at best, distant cousins. This chapter covers a few of the more popular members of this extended query family.

Becoming Annoyingly Efficient with Update Queries

Back in Chapter 14, "The Needle in a Haystack Thing: Finding and Sorting Data," you learned how to use the Replace command to make global changes to a field. While this command often comes in handy, there are some jobs it just can't handle. For example, what if you wanted to replace the contents of a field with a new value, but only for records that meet certain criteria? Or what if your table includes price data and you want to increase all the prices by 5%?

Queries that make changes to a table are called **action queries**.

For these tasks, you need a more sophisticated tool: an *update query*. Unlike a select query, which only displays a subset of the table, an update query actually makes changes to the table data. The idea is that you select a field to work with, specify the new field value, set up some criteria (this is optional), and then run the query. Access flashes through the table and changes the field entries to the new value. If you entered criteria, only records that match the criteria are updated.

To create an update query, first create a select query that includes the field (or fields) you want to update and the field (or fields) you'll need for the criteria. (Remember, criteria are optional for an update query. If you leave them out, Access will update every record in the table.) When the select query is complete, run it to make sure the criteria are working properly.

To convert the query to an update query, pull down the **Query** menu, and select the **Update** command. Access changes the title bar to Update Query and replaces the QBE grid's **Sort** and **Show** lines with an **Update To** line. Select the **Update To** cell for the field you want to change, and enter the new value. The following picture shows an example update query for a Products table. Here, the Discount field will be changed to 0.45 for those products with a Category ID of 7.

 Click on this button in the toolbar to convert a query into an update query.

```
┌─────────────────────────────────────────────┐
│  ─        Update Query: Discount Adjustment    ▼ ▲ │
│  ┌──────────┐                                      │
│  │ Products │                                      │
│  │Units On Order ▲                                 │
│  │Unit Price│                                       │
│  │Reorder Level                                     │
│  │Discontinued                                      │
│  │Category ID                                       │
│  │Discount  ▼                                       │
│  └──────────┘                                      │
│  ┌─┐                                         ┌─┐   │
│  │◄│                                         │►│   │
│  └─┘                                         └─┘   │
│  ┌──────────────────────────────────────────────┐ │
│  │ Field:  │Discount   │Category ID │          │▲│ │
│  │Update To:│0.45      │            │          │ │ │
│  │ Criteria:│          │7           │          │ │ │
│  │     or:  │          │            │          │▼│ │
│  └─┴────────┴──────────┴────────────┴──────────┘ │
└─────────────────────────────────────────────┘
```

An update query that changes the Discount field to 0.45 for products where the Category ID is 7.

When the query is ready, select the **Query** menu's **Run** command. Access displays a dialog box to tell you how many records (rows) will be updated. Select **OK**, or press **Enter** to perform the update.

Don't forget you can also click on this button in the toolbar to run a query.

Once you see what update queries can do, you'll wonder how you ever got along without them. For example, one common table chore is changing prices, and in a large table, it's a drudgery most of us can live without. However, if you're increasing prices by a certain percentage, you can automate the whole process with an update query. For example, suppose you want to increase each value in a Price field by 5%. To handle this in an update query, you'd add the Price field to the QBE grid and then enter the following expression in the Update To cell:

Besides multiplication, you can also update numeric or currency fields using addition (+), subtraction (-), and division (/).

[Price]*1.05

Enclosing Price in square brackets ([]) tells Access you're dealing with the Price field. So multiplying this by 1.05 signifies that you want every Price field entry increased by 5%. (You can also, of course, set up criteria to gain even more control over the update.)

Nuking Records with Delete Queries

If you need to delete one or two records from a table, it's easy enough just to select each record and choose the Edit menu's Delete command (as explained back in Chapter 10). But what if you have a large chunk of records to get rid of? For example, if you sell your prized collection of 8-track tapes, then you'll want to delete all the 8-track records from your music database. Similarly, you might want to clean out an Orders table by deleting any old orders that were placed before a certain date. In both examples, you can set up criteria to identify the group of records to delete. You then enter the criteria in a delete query, and Access will delete all the matching records.

Before setting up the delete query, you need to create a select query with the following fields:

☞ The asterisk "field" (the asterisk represents the entire table). With your mouse, drag the asterisk from the top of the field list into the first Field cell in the QBE grid. With your keyboard, drop-down the list of fields in the first Field cell, and select the item that ends with the ".*" symbols. For example, if your table is called Music Collection, "Music Collection.*" is the item you select.

☞ Any field you need for your deletion criteria.

Enter the criteria, and then run the select query to make sure the query is picking out the correct records. If things look okay, you're ready to create the delete query. Return to the query design window, pull down the **Query** menu, and select the **Delete** command. The title bar changes to Delete Query, and Access replaces the Sort and Show lines with a Delete line. The asterisk field will display **"From"** in the Delete cell, and each criteria field will display **"Where"** in the Delete cell.

OOPS!

Always make sure you try out the select query before you even think about moving on to the deletion. The records you'll be deleting will be gone for good, and no amount of huffing and puffing will bring them back. Running the select query is an easy way to prevent wiping out anything important.

 Clicking on this button in the toolbar converts a query into a delete query.

Delete Query: Delete 8-Tracks

Music Collection

*
MusicCollectionID
ArtistID
CategoryID
GroupName
Title

Field:	Music Collection.*	Format
Delete:	From	Where
Criteria:		"8-Track"
or:		

A delete query uses the asterisk field and any fields you need for your criteria.

When you're ready, take a deep breath, and select **Run** from the **Query** menu. Access analyzes the criteria and then displays a dialog box telling you how many records you'll be deleting. If the number seems reasonable, select **OK**, or press **Enter** to proceed.

Giving Birth to New Tables with Make Table Queries

As I explained back in Chapter 17, the results of select queries are called *dynasets* because they are dynamic subsets of the table data. When I say "dynamic," I mean that if you edit the query records, the corresponding records in the table also change. Similarly, if you edit the table, Access changes the query records automatically.

This is usually welcome behavior because at least you know you're always working with the most up-to-date information. However, there may be the odd time when this is not the behavior you want. For example, at the end of the month or the end of the fiscal year, you might want some of your tables to be "frozen" while you tie things up for month- or year-end (this would apply particularly to tables that track invoices).

Instead of letting the new work pile up until the table can be released, Access lets you create a table from an existing one. You could then use the new table for your month-end duties, so the old table doesn't need to be held up. You do this using a *make table* query.

As usual, you begin by creating a select query that includes the fields you want for the new table as well as any criteria you need. (Be sure to run the select query to make sure the fields and records displayed are the ones you want.) Then pull down the **Query** menu, and select the Make Table command. Access displays the Query Properties dialog box, shown on the following page. In the Table Name text box, enter the name you want to use for the new table. When you're done, select **OK**, or press **Enter**.

 You can also start a make table query by clicking on this button in the toolbar.

The Query Properties dialog box.

Select **Run** from the **Query** menu to start the query. Access displays a dialog box to let you know how many records will be copied into the new table. Select **OK**, or press **Enter** to create the new table.

Version 2.0's Query Wizard Queries

With the Query Wizards, you have access to four other types of queries and, perhaps best of all, you don't have to mess around with the query design window. The Query Wizards let you create each query in the usual step-by-step Wizard method that we've come to know and love.

You begin by creating a new query object. Just to refresh your memory, you can use any of the following techniques:

- ☞ Pull down the **File** menu, select **New**, and then select **Query**.

- ☞ Select the database window's **Query** tab, and then select the **New** button.

- ☞ Click on the **New Query** button in the toolbar.

The New Query button.

In the New Query dialog box that appears, select the Query **Wizards** button. Access displays a dialog box that lists the four Query Wizards. Highlight the Wizard you want, and then select **OK** to continue. You can then follow the instructions in each Wizard dialog box to create your query. The next four sections describe each of the four Query Wizard types.

To learn how to use the various Wizard buttons you'll be seeing, refer to Chapter 8, "Using Version 2.0's Handy Table Wizard," to get the details.

The row-and-column summary is called a **cross-tabulation**, or **crosstab**, for short.

Crosstab Queries

Crosstab queries take large amounts of complex data and summarize some or all of the information into a handy row-and-column format.

For example, consider the Sales Promotion Orders table shown next. This table lists orders taken during a sales promotion. The customer could select any one of four products (copy holder, glare filter, mouse pad, printer stand) and two promotions (1 Free with 10, Extra Discount).

Date	Product	Quantity	Net $	Promotion
6/1/94	Printer stand	11	$119.70	1 Free with 10
6/1/94	Glare filter	6	$77.82	Extra Discount
6/1/94	Mouse pad	15	$100.95	Extra Discount
6/1/94	Glare filter	11	$149.71	1 Free with 10
6/2/94	Mouse pad	22	$155.40	1 Free with 10
6/2/94	Mouse pad	3	$20.19	Extra Discount
6/2/94	Copy holder	5	$33.65	Extra Discount
6/2/94	Printer stand	22	$239.36	1 Free with 10
6/2/94	Glare filter	10	$129.70	Extra Discount
6/3/94	Mouse pad	22	$155.40	1 Free with 10
6/3/94	Printer stand	8	$82.96	Extra Discount
6/3/94	Printer stand	22	$239.40	1 Free with 10
6/3/94	Copy holder	55	$388.50	1 Free with 10
6/3/94	Mouse pad	25	$168.25	Extra Discount
6/3/94	Glare filter	22	$299.42	1 Free with 10
6/6/94	Printer stand	11	$119.70	1 Free with 10

Table: Sales Promotion Orders — Record: 1 of 240

A table of orders taken during a promotion.

A basic analysis of this table would be to calculate how many of each product were ordered for each promotion. With over 200 orders, this would be a nightmare to figure out by hand, but a crosstab query (like the one that follows) does the job nicely. In this case, Access took the four unique entries in the Product field and used them as entries in the leftmost column, and it took the two unique entries in the Promotion field and used them as headings for the other columns. It then summed the appropriate Quantity field values and—presto!—summarized everything in a nice, neat package.

Crosstab Query: Sales Promotio		
Product	1 Free with 10	Extra Discount
Copy holder	792	647
Glare filter	814	894
Mouse pad	1705	1655
Printer stand	638	706
Record: 1	of 4	

The table data presented as a crosstab query.

The Crosstab Query Wizard asks you to pick a table and then do the following:

☛ Select a field whose unique entries will appear in the leftmost column of the query.

☛ Select a field whose unique entries will appear as the headings for the other columns in the query.

☛ Select a field to use for the calculations and the type of calculation to use (such as Sum, Count).

☛ Assign a name to the query.

Find Duplicates Queries

If you're concerned about having duplicate records in a table, a Find Duplicates query will scope them out for you. This query displays a list of a table's duplicate entries (if it has any). You can then use this information to return to the table and either edit or delete one or more records to remove the duplication.

After you select the table you want to use, the Find Duplicates Query Wizard then takes you through the following tasks:

☛ Selecting one or more fields that may contain duplicate information (you can select up to 10 fields).

☛ Selecting any other fields you want to see in the query.

☛ Naming the query.

Find Unmatched Queries

The Find Unmatched Query Wizard lets you find records in one table that have no matching entries in another. For example, suppose you have a Products table (with a Product ID field) and an Orders table (also with a Product ID field). This Wizard can examine both tables and, using the common Product ID field as a guide, tell you if any records in the Products table have no matching records in the Orders table. In other words, it gives you a list of the products that have not been ordered.

When you start this Wizard, it asks you to select the table you want to see in the query results. In the above example, you'd select the Products table. The next step is to select the table that contains the related records (this would be the Orders table, in the example). You then have to do the following:

☛ Select the fields in each table that contain the matching information (for example, Product ID).

☛ Select the fields you want to see in the query.

☛ Enter a name for the query.

Archive Queries

To *archive* records means to remove them from one table and store them in another. This is handy if you have a table with many old records and you want to clean things out to make it easier to navigate and work with the table. One way to do this would be to use a make table query to copy the old records and then a delete query to remove them. While this works well enough, Access has an Archive Query Wizard that makes things that much easier.

As usual, you begin by selecting the table you want to use. You're then taken through the following four procedures:

☛ Enter the criteria that define the records to be archived. You're given three boxes: one for the field name (this is usually a date field), one for the operator (you'll usually select either < or <=), and one for the value (this is usually the date to use as a cutoff).

☛ Examine the records that will be archived to make sure your criteria is correct.

☛ Select whether you want to delete or keep the original records.

☛ Enter a name for the query.

The Least You Need to Know

This chapter showed you numerous examples of queries you can exploit in the real world for fun and profit. Time to check out a few reverse-angle replays:

☛ Use update queries to make criteria-based changes to a table. Select **Update** from the **Query** menu.

☛ Delete queries use criteria to delete records from a table. Select the **Query** menu's **Delete** command.

☛ To make a new table from an existing one, use a make table query. Select the **Query** menu's **Make Table** command.

☛ The Query Wizards let you create four different kinds of queries: crosstab, find duplicates, find unmatched, and archive.

This blank page stuff is really getting out of hand.

Part V
Impressing Friends and Family with Access Reports

"The least you can do is look respectable." My mother, wise woman that she is, gave me that advice when I was young, and I haven't forgotten it. (Of course, I haven't always followed it either, but that's another story!) If looking respectable is your goal, as well, then reports are a must. Reports can take even the frumpiest data and turn it into a thing of beauty. And the bonus is, as you'll see when you read the two chapters in Part V, that it's all very easy to do.

Chapter 20
Diving In: Creating a Report

In This Chapter

- ☛ Learning about reports
- ☛ Creating reports lightning fast with AutoReport
- ☛ Getting friendly with the Report Wizard
- ☛ Creating your own report
- ☛ Printing a report
- ☛ A report fashion show for the clothes horses in the crowd

Most of the work you do with Access—whether it's creating tables, entering data, sorting, filtering, or querying—is work that, generally speaking, you do for yourself. It's valuable work, to be sure, but it's really just "behind-the-scenes" stuff. Reports, though, are like your coming-out party. A report takes your shabby data and polishes it to a handsome shine for all to see. This chapter shows you how to create reports. We'll be looking at three methods: AutoReport, the Report Wizards, and creating a report from scratch.

Reports: Your Data's New Clothes

Before you enter it into an Access table, your data is, essentially, naked. It passes its days exposed to the elements, shivering and cold. To prevent your data from catching its death, you need to cover it in the trappings of a table structure.

But while these new garments may be warm, they aren't much to look at. I mean, let's face it, a datasheet just doesn't present your data in the best light. We're definitely talking Worst Dressed List, here. You can try a little customizing or some sorting as a way of mixing and matching outfits, but these are only cosmetic solutions.

However, this really doesn't matter for those times when you're just kicking around the database house. When you're working with your data, you usually don't care how it looks. But, what about when it's time to go out on the town? What do you do when you need to show your work in a presentation or distribute it to others? Heck, you can't send your data out looking like *that*!

For these special times, you need to dress up your data in clothes appropriate for the occasion. You need, in short, a *report*. A report is a database object that organizes and formats your table or query data to make it presentable and meaningful to other people. With reports, you can organize data into groups, display subtotals and grand totals for appropriate fields, and add lines, graphics, and fonts to put your data at the height of fashion. Best of all, the AutoReport and Query Wizards make creating reports a breeze (although you can also design your own reports from scratch).

Quick and Dirty Reports with Version 2.0's AutoReport

Got a meeting in five minutes and need a report for your data? No problem. Access version 2.0's AutoReport feature will create a simple report for you in just a few seconds. Here's how it works. First, select the table or query you want to work with. If the table or query is already open, that's fine. Otherwise, select either the **Table** or **Query** tab in the database window, and then highlight the object you want to use.

When you're ready, simply click on the **AutoReport** button in the toolbar. Access ruminates for a bit and then displays a report like the following one. If you need to print out your report, see "Printing a Report," later in this chapter.

 The AutoReport button.

Report: March Transactions					

Checking Account

4/1/94

ID	Date	Check Number	Payee	Withdrawal	Deposit
1	3/1/94	1	Crazy Al's Meats	$32.97	
2	3/2/94	2	Shyster & Son, Attorneys at Law	$500.00	
3	3/3/94	3	Fly By Night Travel	$1,237.50	
4	3/7/94		Withdrawal	$100.00	

Page: 1

A simple report generated by AutoReport.

Checking Out the Report Wizards

For more sophisticated reports, you'll need to turn to the Report Wizards. There are seven in all, and they can generate handy reports that do things such as group and total data, calculate summaries, and create mailing labels.

BY THE WAY

If you don't have access to the toolbar (if, say, you don't have a mouse), you can still generate a quick report with the AutoReport Wizard. For details, read on.

Getting Started

Before starting a Report Wizard, you need to create a report object. Here are the three methods you can use:

☞ Pull down the File menu, select New, and then select **Report**.

☞ In the database window, select the **Report** tab, and then select the New button.

☞ Click on the **New Report** button in the toolbar.

 The New Report button.

If you've never used an Access Wizard before (or if you need your memory refreshed), hike back to Chapter 8, "Using Version 2.0's Handy Table Wizard," to find out what all those Wizard dialog box buttons are for.

In each case, Access displays the New Report dialog box. In the Select a Table/Query drop-down box, select the table or query you want to use in the report. Then, select the Report Wizards button. Access displays a list of the Report Wizards. Select the Wizard you want to work with, and then select **OK**, or press **Enter**.

The next few sections discuss most (but not all) of the Report Wizards.

Creating a Single-Column Report

The *single-column* report displays the fields in a single column down the middle of the page. This is useful for tables or queries that have a large number of fields (since you might not be able to display all the fields across a single page). The disadvantage is that you'll get fewer records on each page.

The Single-Column Report Wizard starts you off by asking which fields you want to include in the report. You're then taken through the following procedures:

☞ Select the field (or fields) to use for sorting the report.

☞ Select a report style: Executive, Presentation, or Ledger. You can also select an orientation (Portrait or Landscape) and the spacing between the report lines.

☞ Enter a title for the report. You can also choose to print each record on a new page and whether or not the title appears on each page.

Creating a Groups/Totals Report

A *groups/totals* report is one of the most useful of the Wizard reports. The *groups* part means the Wizard divides your table or query data into groups of related records. In an invoice table, for example, you could group the invoices by customer name or due date. The *totals* part means the Wizard creates subtotals for each group and an overall total for the report. These totals are created for each numeric field you include in the report. In the invoice table, for example, you could get totals for the invoice amount. The picture below shows a sample of a groups/totals report.

A groups/totals report for a table of invoices.

The Groups/Totals Report Wizard begins by asking you to select the fields to include in the report. The Wizard then subjects you to several dialog boxes that ask you to do the following:

- ☛ Select the field (or fields) you want to use as the basis for the report groups.

- ☛ Select the grouping you want to use (you'll usually select Normal).

- ☛ Select a style for the report.

- ☛ Enter a title and other options.

Creating a Mailing Label Report

A *mailing label* report does just about what you'd expect: it creates a report of names and addresses suitable for printing on mailing labels. *Here's* a sample mailing label report.

A mailing label report.

When you start the Mailing Label Report Wizard, the first dialog box lets you choose the fields you want on your mailing labels and define the layout of each label. Here are the steps to follow to design your label:

1. Add a field to the label.

2. Add any punctuation you need by clicking on one of the buttons below the field list. You can add a colon (:), a comma (,), a dash (-), a period (.), a slash (/), or a space.

3. Repeat steps 1 and 2 until the line is set up the way you want. For example, if your table includes first and last names in separate fields, you'd add the first name field, add a space, and then add the last name field.

4. Click on the **NewLine** button to start a new line.

5. Repeat steps 1–4 until the label design is complete.

The Wizard then guides you through the following steps:

- ☞ Select a sort order for the labels.
- ☞ Select a label size and label type.
- ☞ Select a font and color for the label text.

Creating a Summary Report (Version 2.0 Only)

A *summary* report doesn't show individual records. Instead, it groups records together according to a field you specify and then shows only the group totals (as well as a grand total) for each numeric field you include in the report. The Summary Report Wizard is almost identical to the Groups/Totals Report Wizard.

Creating a Tabular Report (Version 2.0 Only)

A *tabular* report displays the data in a table format. Each field appears in its own column, and each record takes up a single line of the report. The Tabular Report Wizard is almost identical to the Single-Column Report Wizard.

Creating an AutoReport (Version 2.0 Only)

This one's a no-brainer. The AutoReport Wizard simply creates the same report you get when you run the AutoReport feature. Once you select this Wizard, just stand back and let Access take over.

Creating Your Own Report from Scratch

If the Report Wizard reports don't quite cut the mustard for you, you can create your own reports by hand. This takes a little more effort, but the upside is that you get a report that suits your needs exactly.

Building a new report from scratch may not be the best way to go. If the report you need is similar to one of the Report Wizard formats, a much better plan would be to create the Wizard report, and then customize it the way you want. Chapter 21, "Getting Fancy: Customizing a Report," tells you everything you need to know.

To create your own report, begin by creating a new report object using any of the following techniques:

☞ Select the File menu's New command, and then select **Report**.

☞ Select the database window's **Report** tab, and then select the New button.

☞ Click on the toolbar's **New Report** button.

 The New Report button.

In the New Report dialog box, use the Select a Table/Query drop-down list to select the table or query you want to use in the report. Then, select the **Blank Report button. Access displays the report design window, which looks like this:

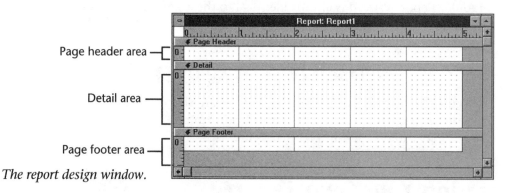

Page header area —
Detail area —
Page footer area —

The report design window.

The report design window is divided into the following three areas:

Page Header   The controls you enter into this area appear at the top of each page of the report. For example, if you'll be placing your fields in columns, you could use this area for the field names.

Detail   You'll use this area to hold the fields you want to include in your report.

Page Footer   This area appears at the bottom of each page of the report. This is useful for things like page numbers (see Chapter 21).

Adding Controls to the Report

You create a report by adding labels and fields to the design window and arranging them into the format you want. I won't go into the details here, because the techniques are exactly the same as those you learned for form design (see Chapter 13, "Improving Your Form"). If you want to learn how to add a report title and how to sort and group the report records, these subjects (and more) are covered in Chapter 21.

Seeing a Preview of the Report

If you want to get a look at your report while designing it, select the File menu's Sample Preview command. Access removes the design elements and shows you what the report will look like. When you're done admiring your handiwork, select the Sample Preview command again. Access returns you to the design window.

 Click on this button in the Report Design toolbar to see a preview of your report.

Saving a Report

As soon as possible after creating a report, you should save it. Just pull down the File menu, and select the Save command. If this is your first time saving the report, Access displays the Save As dialog box. Use the Report Name text box to enter a name for the report, and then select **OK**, or press **Enter**.

Printing a Report

Reports, more than any other database object, are designed to be printed. After all, their main purpose in life is to make your data comprehensible to other people. So, to disseminate your work of art to family, friends, and colleagues, you need to print it out. Happily, this isn't hard to do. With the report displayed (or highlighted in the Table tab of the database window), pull down the File menu, and select the **Print** command (or press **Ctrl+P** in version 2.0). Access displays the Print dialog box. Use the Copies

Before printing, make sure your printer is turned on and that it has plenty of paper.

text box to enter the number of copies you want, and then select **OK**, or press **Enter**.

 You can also display the Print dialog box by clicking on this button in the toolbar.

The Least You Need to Know

This chapter got you started with Access reports. I'll be showing you how to customize your reports in the next chapter, but let's take stock of this chapter's main points before moving on:

☞ Reports are to your data what tuxedos and evening gowns are to social gadabouts.

☞ To get a quick report, select a table or query, and then click on the **AutoReport** button in the toolbar.

☞ The Report Wizards can create six different kinds of reports: single-column, groups/totals, mailing label, summary, tabular, and an AutoReport.

☞ To start a Report Wizard, create a new report object, select Report **W**izards from the New Report dialog box, and then select the Wizard you want.

☞ To create your own report, create a new report object, and then select **B**lank Report from the New Report dialog box.

☞ To print a report, pull down the **F**ile menu's **P**rint command, enter the number of copies you want in the **C**opies text box, and then select **OK**.

Chapter 21

Getting Fancy: Customizing a Report

In This Chapter

☞ Working with report sections

☞ Adding a title to a report

☞ Sorting and grouping data

☞ Adding page numbers, the date and time, and totals

☞ Rambling ruminations on creating ravishingly readable reports

As you saw in the last chapter, AutoReport and the Report Wizards make creating great-looking reports a breeze. However, as you're getting used to these tools, you may make a mistake or two: for example, you may forget a field or select an incorrect option. Rather than suffering in silence with a not-quite-perfect report, you can customize the darn thing to bring it up to your usual standards. As you'll see in this chapter, when you customize a report you can move elements around, add new ones, sort and group your data, and just generally have fun playing with the look and feel of your budding work of art. Just don't forget us little people when you become a star!

Basic Customization Chores (Or: The Author Passes the Buck)

Chapter 13, "Improving Your Form," showed you a fistful of ways to whip your forms into shape. This included such basic chores as selecting, moving, and sizing controls; adding labels and fields; changing fonts; and working with colors and borders. If you've read that chapter, the good news is that pretty well everything you learned applies to reports, as well. If you didn't read Chapter 13, then the bad news is that I won't be covering these techniques again in this chapter. Bummer.

But that's okay, though, because it gives us some extra room to check out a few report-specific goodies. In particular, we'll cover the following topics in this chapter:

- ☞ Adding a title to a report
- ☞ Sorting and grouping your data
- ☞ Inserting dates and page numbers
- ☞ Adding calculations

If you want to learn how to add lines, boxes, and other graphic objects to your report, see Chapter 23, "Image is Everything: Using Graphics in Tables."

Opening the Report Design Window

As you saw in the last chapter, Access reports have a *design view* you can use for your customization tasks. To display this view, try either of these methods:

- ☞ If you're in the database window, highlight the report in the Report tab, and then select the Design button.

- ☞ If the report is open in the preview screen, pull down the File menu, and select the Sample Preview command.

Working with Report Sections

Before getting down to the nitty-gritty of report customization, you should know a thing or two about working with the report design sections (Page Header, Detail, and Page Footer). Basically, you need to know two things: how to select a section and how to change the size of a section.

Selecting a Section

To select a section, all you do is click on the bar above the section (that is, the area that holds the name of the section). Access highlights the bar to tell you the section is selected.

Why would you want to select a section? One common reason is to change the background color of the section (see Chapter 13 to learn how to work with colors). You just select the section and then choose a background color from the Palette tool.

Another reason is to move a control from one section to another. As you learned in Chapter 13, you can move most controls by dragging the control's move handle. In the report design window, however, this doesn't always work. For example, you can't drag a field label from the Detail section to the Page Header section. Instead, you have to select the label, choose the Edit menu's Cut command, select the Page Header section, and then choose Paste from the Edit menu.

Changing the Size of a Section

Section sizes can play a large role in report design. For example, the size of the Detail section usually determines how much space appears between each record in your report. If this section is too large, your lines will be too far apart. Here are the techniques to use to change the size of a section:

☛ To change the height of a section, move the mouse pointer to the bottom of the section until the pointer changes to a horizontal line with two arrows protruding from the top and bottom. The picture below shows the mouse pointer positioned for changing the height of the Detail section. Now press and hold the left mouse button, and drag the pointer up (to make the section smaller) or down (to make it larger).

☛ To change the width of all the sections, move the mouse pointer to the right edge of any one of the sections. The pointer changes to a vertical line with arrows on the left and right. Drag the pointer left (to make the sections smaller) or right (to make them larger).

The mouse pointer positioned correctly for adjusting the height of the Detail section.

The mouse pointer for changing the height of a section

Adding a Report Title

The Report Wizards automatically add titles to the reports they create, but if you're building your own report, you'll need to create the title yourself.

The first thing you need to do is create a Report Header section to hold the title. This section appears only at the top of the first page of the report. You add it by selecting the Format menu's Report Header/Footer command (in version 1.1, select the Layout menu's Report Hdr/Ftr command). Access adds both a Report Header and Report Footer section.

Now add a label to the Report Header section, enter the title text you want to use, and format the label appropriately (this is all covered in Chapter 13). The following picture shows a report with a title added.

![Report: A/R Report design view showing Report Header with "Accounts Receivable Invoices Report" title, Page Header with Customer Name:, Invoice #:, Amount: labels, Detail section, Page Footer, and Report Footer sections]

A report with a title added to the Report Header section.

You may be wondering how I managed to underline the title in the report shown here. Well, it's not hard, but it's not obvious either (Access has a nasty habit of hiding things like this). First, select the label, and then choose the **V**iew menu's **P**roperties command. In the dialog box that appears, select **Layout Properties** from the drop-down list, and then, in the Font Underline property, select **Yes**. Press **Alt+F4** to exit the dialog box.

Sorting and Grouping Report Data

As you saw in the last chapter, the Groups/Totals Report Wizard creates a report that shows the table or query data sorted and grouped according to the entries in one of the fields. This is a great way to turn a confusing jumble of records into a comprehensible document.

You can add this same advantage to just about any report by using Access' sorting and grouping feature. To start this feature, pull down the **V**iew menu, and select the **S**orting and Grouping command. You'll see the Sorting and Grouping dialog box.

Clicking on this button in the toolbar will also display the Sorting and Grouping dialog box.

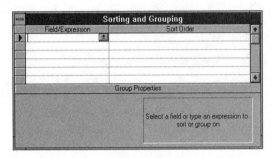

The Sorting and Grouping dialog box.

Another way to display the Sorting and Grouping dialog box is to right-click on any empty part of the design area and then select the **Sorting and Grouping** command from the shortcut menu.

Setting Up Sorting Options

You use the top half of the Sorting and Grouping dialog box to define the sort order you want for your report. Select the first **Field/Expression** cell, drop-down the list (by clicking on the arrow or by pressing **Alt+down arrow**), and then select the name of the field you want to sort on. In the Sort Order cell, select either **Ascending** or **Descending**.

Setting Up Grouping Options

A *group* is simply a collection of related records. In an invoice table report, for example, you could create groups of invoices for each customer. I know what you're thinking: sorting arranges similar records so they appear together, so why do we need groups? Well, the advantage you get with groups is that Access creates two new report sections: a *group header* and a *group footer*. You can use a header to identify the group and the footer to print summary information about the group (such as a total or other calculation; see "Working With Report Expressions," later in this chapter).

To group your report on a field, first select the field in the top half of the Sorting and Grouping dialog box. You'll see a list of properties appear for the field in the bottom half of the dialog box. To add a group header, select **Yes** in the Group Header property. To add a group footer, select **Yes** in the Group Footer property.

When you exit the dialog box (by pressing **Alt+F4**), you'll see the new group header and group footer sections added to the report, as in the example that follows. Be sure to add any text or expressions you need to the header or footer. (In the picture, I've added the field name into the Customer Name Header section.)

A report with a group header and footer added.

Working with Report Expressions

Until now, you've been using text boxes to hold table or query field data. But text boxes have other uses, as well. In particular, you can use them to add *expressions* to your reports. In a nutshell, an expression is a calculation of one kind or another. For example, if you have a numeric field in your report, you could add an expression that calculates the sum of that field. You can also use expressions to add page numbers, the current date or time, or a count of the records in the report.

Adding Page Numbers

One of the common expressions that people most often add to their reports is the page number. Of course, if your report is only a page or two long, this won't be a big deal. But if you're dealing with a few pages or more, page numbers become an almost essential way to keep things in order once the report is printed.

To add page numbers to your report, create a text box control inside the Page Footer section, and then type **=Page** inside the text box. Here, **Page** is a built-in Access function that automatically keeps track of your report's page numbers.

Many people like their page numbering to use the format **Page x of y**. This tells people they're reading, for example, page **7** of a report that has a total of **22** pages. Access has another function—**Pages**—that calculates the total number of pages in a report. To get the above format, then, you'd enter the following into a text box:

="Page " & Page & " of " & Pages

The stuff in quotes is just plain text, and all those ampersand things (**&**) tell Access to combine everything into a single phrase.

Adding Dates or Times

A report is a snapshot of a table or query taken at a given time, so it often helps to know when the report was generated. To do this, Access lets you add dates or times (or both) to your reports.

Adding dates or times is similar to adding page numbers. You create a text box and then enter one of the functions listed here:

Type	To Get
=Date()	The current date
=Time()	The current time
=Now()	Both the date and time (in that order)

Adding Calculations

You can also use expressions to perform calculations involving one or more fields. For example, if you have a table of orders, you could multiply the quantity ordered times the price to get the extended price for that item. Similarly, Access has functions that can add up the numbers in a particular field, count the records in the report, and more.

To enter a simple calculation in a text box, you begin, as usual, with an equal sign (=). You then combine one or more field names with the operators. You enclose the field names in square brackets. Here are the Access arithmetic operators:

Use	*For*
+	Addition
-	Subtraction
*	Multiplication
/	Division

BY THE WAY

By default, Access displays dates in the Short Date (**MM/DD/YY**) format and times in the Long Time (**HH:MM:SS AM/PM**) format. To change these formats, first select the text box, then pull down the **View** menu, and choose the **Properties** command. In the dialog box that appears, select Data Properties from the drop-down list, and then use the Format property to select the format you want. Press **Alt+F4** to return to the window.

For example, to multiply a field named **Quantity** by another field named **Price**, you'd enter the following expression in a text box inside your report's Detail section:

=[Quantity]*[Price]

Access' arithmetic functions work slightly differently from arithmetic expressions, however. The functions don't need operators; you type the name of the function followed by the field name (in square brackets) surrounded by parentheses. Hunh? Let's look at an example. Suppose your table has a field called **Amount** and you want to display the sum of the entries in that field for all the records in the report. This is a job for the Sum( ) function, so you'd enter the following expression into a text box inside the Report Footer section:

=Sum([Amount])

If you enter a calculation in the Report Footer, Access performs the calculation over the entire report. If the calculation is in a group footer or page footer, Access calculates with only those records included in the group or page.

Other functions you can use include Avg( ) (which calculates the average value in a field), Count( ) (which tells you the number of records in the table or query), Max( ) (which tells you the maximum value in a field), and Min( ) (which—you guessed it—tells you the minimum value in a field).

The following picture shows a report that uses a couple of calculations (and some other expressions).

A report with several expressions scattered willy-nilly.

The Least You Need to Know

This chapter gave you the poop on customizing your reports. Here's a customized version of the important stuff:

- ☞ To open the report design window, highlight the report in the database window, and select the **Design** button.

- ☞ To add a report title, activate the **Format** menu's Report **Header/Footer** command, and add a label inside the new Report Header section.

- ☞ To sort and group the report data, select **Sorting** and **Grouping** from the **View** menu.

- ☞ You can use text boxes for expressions instead of just fields. Common expressions include **=page** for page numbers, **=date( )** for the current date, and **=time( )** for the current time.

- ☞ To create arithmetic expressions, combine one or more field names enclosed in square brackets with the arithmetic operators. You can also use functions, such as Sum( ), Avg( ), and Count( ).

**This page really isn't blank-
it just looks that way.**

Part VI

Access Excess: Advanced Topics for the Brave (or Foolhardy)

Access follows the old "80–20" rule: you'll spend 80% of your time using 20% of its features. Because of this, we've spent most of our time in this book concentrating on the 20% of Access you'll be using most often. But what about the other 80%? Surely, there must be something there that would appeal to more than just Access techno-geeks. Well, happily, there are a few gems that can be mined to make your Access life easier and more productive. Part VI looks at three of them: getting control over Access by setting a few program options; using graphics in your tables, forms, and reports; and working with multiple tables.

Chapter 22
Personalizing Access' Program Options

In This Chapter

- ☞ Working with Access' general program options
- ☞ Changing the behavior of the keyboard
- ☞ Customizing your datasheets
- ☞ Setting toolbar options
- ☞ Umpteen ways to personalize Access to suit your tastebuds

One of the fast-food burger chains has carved out a sizable niche for itself by advertising that you can "have it your way." This means you actually have a choice about which toppings appear on your burger. Access, too, lets you "have it your way." In this case, the "toppings" you're dealing with let you control the program's default settings for your keyboard, the toolbars, the datasheet, and more. Many of these options are absurdly technical, but most are downright useful. This chapter looks at the useful ones and tells you how they can make your Access life tastier. Bon appetit!

Displaying the Options Dialog Box

All the program options we'll be dealing with can be found in the Options dialog box shown in the following figure. To display this dialog box, you need to open a database and then select the View menu's Options command. (This command is also available from any datasheet, form, query, or report.)

You'll be using the Options dialog box to customize Access.

This dialog box has two areas:

Category   A list of customization categories.

Items   A list of options and properties you can set. The list you see depends on the category you've selected. Most of the items are drop-down lists or text boxes.

When you've finished setting your options, select **OK**, or press **Enter** to put them into effect.

Setting the General Options

The General category is a catch-all list of options and properties that cover everything from displaying the status bar to the turning various confirmations on or off. There are no less than 18 available options, not all of which are particularly beneficial (or even comprehensible). Here's a run-down of the ones you need to worry about:

Show Status Bar   To get a slightly bigger screen area, you can set this item to **No** to hide the status bar. Otherwise, select **Yes** to display the status bar.

Built-In Toolbars Available   If you don't use the toolbars, you can get back even more screen real estate by setting this option to **No**. This hides all of the Access toolbars. Select **Yes** to display the toolbars.

Confirm Document Deletions   You can delete any database object by highlighting it in the database window and selecting the Edit menu's Delete command (or you can just press the **Delete** key). When you set this item to **Yes**, Access always displays a dialog box that asks you to confirm the deletion. Some folks don't like this distrustful attitude, so they change this option to **No**.

Confirm Action Queries   As you learned back in Chapter 19, "More Members of the Query Family," action queries are queries that make changes to a table (or create a new one). These include update queries, delete queries, and make table queries. If the Confirm Action Queries option is set to **Yes**, Access displays a dialog box telling you how many records will be affected by the action query. Changing this setting to **No** turns off these dialog boxes.

I highly recommend leaving the Confirm Document Deletions option set to **Yes**. A deleted object is gone for good, so if the confirmation prevents even one accidental deletion, it's easily worth the slight hassle it creates.

Confirm Record Changes   When this setting is **Yes**, Access displays a dialog box asking for confirmation when you delete or paste records, or make changes with the Replace command. Selecting **No**, instead, turns off these confirmations (although, again, I don't recommend this).

The last three items in version 2.0's General category (Show Tool Tips, Color Buttons on Toolbars, and Large Toolbar Buttons) all deal with the toolbars. See "Changing the Toolbar Options," later in this chapter for an easier way to deal with these settings.

Changing the Keyboard Behavior

The options available in the Keyboard category affect the behavior of the keyboard in datasheets, forms, and select query dynasets. Here's a look at three of the options:

Arrow Key Behavior This option is normally set to Next Field, which means that pressing the left or right arrow key moves you left or right to the next field. (To move left or right one character at a time, you need to press **F2**.) You can also set this option to **Next Character**. This means the left and right arrow keys will move the insertion point left and right one character at a time.

Move After Enter This option controls the behavior of the Enter key. The default value is **Next Field**, which means that pressing **Enter** takes you to the next field to the right. If you set this to **No**, pressing **Enter** only selects the current field. If you set it to **Next Record**, Access always moves to the first field of the next record.

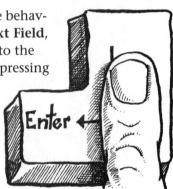

Cursor Stops at First/Last Field This option controls how you navigate a datasheet with your keyboard. Normally (that is, when this setting is **No**), if you press the right arrow key (or **Tab** or **Enter**) when you're on the last field in a record, Access moves to the first field in the next record. Similarly, pressing the left arrow (or **Shift+Tab**) while on the first field moves you to the last field of the previous record. Changing this option to **Yes** tells Access not to move to a new record when you're on either the first or last field in the current record.

Setting the Print Margins

When you print a table or report, the page *margins* are the empty spaces that surround the text on the left, right, top, and bottom. The Printing category lets you make adjustments to the size of these margins. Why would anyone want to do such a thing? Here are a few good reasons:

Before adjusting your margin sizes, it might help to see a preview of the printout so you can see how things will look on the printed page. You can do this by selecting the **File** menu's **Print Preview** command. This displays a window that shows your printout one page at a time.

- ☞ If someone else is going to be making notes on the page, it helps to include bigger left and right margins to give them more room for scribbling.

- ☞ Smaller margins all around mean you get more data on a page. If you have a lot of data, this could save you a few pages when you print it out.

- ☞ If your printout is just slightly longer than a page (say, by only a line or two), you could decrease the top and bottom margins just enough to fit the wayward lines onto a single page.

Some printers (especially laser printers) will choke on really small margins (say, less than 0.25 inches).

The Printing category in the Options dialog box contains the margin values (Left Margin, Right Margin, Top Margin, and Bottom Margin). The default settings are 1 inch for each margin (this means that, on each side of the page, there is one inch of emptiness between the edge of the page and the printed data). You can enter any number between 0 and the width (in the case of the left and right margins) or height (for the top and bottom margins) of the page.

The Printing settings will affect only *new* reports and forms. If you want to adjust the margins on an existing report or form, select the File menu's Print Setup command, and then, in the Print Setup dialog box (as shown here), use the Left, Right, Top, and Bottom text boxes to enter your new margins.

The Print Setup dialog box.

Altering the Look of the Datasheet

You'll probably be spending a lot of time messing about in datasheets, so it makes sense to customize them to suit the way you work. The Datasheet category lets you set the following options for your new datasheets (sorry, these options have no effect on existing datasheets):

Default Gridlines Behavior The *gridlines* are the vertical and horizontal lines that separate the fields and records in the datasheet. Some people think datasheets look neater without these gridlines, so they set this property to **Off**. (To turn off gridlines in an existing datasheet, pull down the Format menu, and select the Gridlines command.)

Default Column Width Access normally creates columns for each field that are one inch wide. If you'd prefer a larger or smaller width, enter a larger or smaller number for this option (you can enter a number between 0 and 22 inches). Chapter 11, "Gaining the Upper Hand on Those Pesky Datasheets," showed you how to adjust column widths in an existing datasheet.

Default Font These settings (Default Font Name, Default Font Size, Default Font Weight, Default Font Italic, and Default Font Underline) determine the font attributes of the datasheet entries. See Chapter 11, "Gaining the Upper Hand on Those Pesky Datasheets," to learn more about these font settings.

The New Datasheet Options dialog box.

Changing the Toolbar Options in Version 2.0

As I mentioned earlier, the General category has a few toolbar options. Although there's nothing wrong with using the Options dialog box to set these properties, Access version 2.0 has a Toolbars dialog box that makes it a bit easier. To display this dialog box, pull down the View menu, and select the Toolbars command. The following Toolbars dialog box appears:

The Toolbars dialog box.

You'll be happy to know you can ignore most of the stuff in this dialog box. The options we care about are at the bottom:

Color Buttons   Many of the toolbar buttons have a splash of color to liven things up. If you don't have a color screen, you may be able to see these buttons better by deactivating this check box to turn off the color.

TECHNO NERD TEACHES...

You usually only need the larger toolbar buttons if you're working in a video mode other than VGA (for example, SuperVGA). How do you know whether you're in VGA or something else? Well, one easy way is to simply look at the toolbar. If the rightmost button is near the right edge of the screen, you're in VGA mode. If there's a large gap between the rightmost button and the right edge of the screen, you're in some higher resolution.

Large Buttons   If you're having trouble seeing the toolbar buttons, activate this check box to increase the size of each button. One caveat, though: increasing the button size may cause some of the buttons to disappear off the right side of the screen. Bad news! There is a solution, however: move the mouse pointer over an empty part of the toolbar, hold down the left mouse button, and then drag the toolbar down into the work area. When you release the button, Access redisplays the toolbar as a rectangular palette (as shown here).

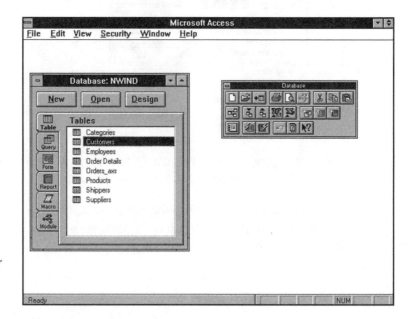

The Database toolbar displayed as a floating palette.

Show ToolTips   As you may know by now, if the mouse pointer lingers over a toolbar button for a second or two, Access pops up a small message called a *ToolTip* that tells you the name of the button. If, for some reason, you'd prefer not to see the ToolTips, deactivate this check box.

The Least You Need to Know

This chapter took you on a ride through Access' dizzying array of program options. Here are a few of my favorite things:

- ☞ To display the Options dialog box, open a database, pull down the **View** menu, and select the **O**ptions command. (You can also select this command from any datasheet, form, query, or report window.)

- ☞ The General options cover items, such as displaying the status bar and confirming certain Access actions (like deleting an object).

- ☞ The Keyboard options affect the behavior of the keyboard navigation keys.

- ☞ Use the Printing category to set up the page margins for all new datasheets and reports.

- ☞ The Datasheet category lets you control the look of the datasheet window for all new tables. You can change the gridline display, the default column width, and the default data font.

- ☞ Pull down the **View** menu, and select the Tool**b**ars command to see a dialog box of toolbar options.

**Aha! Caught you reading a
blank page again.**

Chapter 23

Image Is Everything: Using Graphics in Access

In This Chapter

- ☞ Including graphics in tables
- ☞ Adding graphics to forms and reports
- ☞ Drawing lines and rectangles
- ☞ Graphing table data
- ☞ More fun time-wasting tools that just about guarantee you'll never get your work done

Television has been around for 40-odd years, which means it has had plenty of time to burn itself into our brains and change the cultural landscape forever. The main upshot of this TV revolution (besides the short attention spans) has been that imagery is now paramount. Pictures, by and large, have a greater impact today than words do.

Until now, our approach to Access has been almost entirely word-oriented. And that's as it should be, because the vast majority of your database work will involve text, numbers, and dates in one form or another. However, there's an entire realm of picture-oriented fun that shouldn't be left out of your Access education. This chapter explores this graphical world and shows you how to do things like entering graphics as data, adding graphics to forms and reports, and displaying table data in graph form.

How do you get things like product and employee pictures inside your computer? Good question. The usual way is to use a *scanner*: a machine that reads a photograph or other image and converts it into the digital form that computers know and love.

Entering Graphics Data in Tables

One of the best ways to get visual with your data is to include graphics right in your tables. This is perfect for tables that store, say, product information, because you can include a picture of the product alongside the price, description, and other data. Similarly, a table of employee data could include pictures of each employee.

Creating an OLE Object Field

Of course, you can't just throw in a graphic any old place you like. Access is a real stickler for entering the right type of data in the right type of field. Text has to go in text fields, dates have to go in date fields, and so on. Graphics, too, need a special field type called an *OLE object*. Here, OLE stands for Object Linking and Embedding, and if it sounds complicated, well, you're right, it is. Fortunately, we can safely ignore the details and concentrate on just getting the job done.

So, if you want to add graphics to a table, the first thing you need to do is create a new field that can handle pictures. This is easy enough: in the table design view, enter the field name you want, and then select **OLE Object** from the Data Type drop-down list. (See Chapter 9, "Creating a Table with Your Bare Hands," to learn more about the table design view.)

Once you have your OLE object field ready, you can go ahead and start entering your graphics. In a datasheet, you have two methods you can use:

- ☞ Copy the graphic image from another application.
- ☞ Create a new graphic from within Access.

Copying a Graphic from Another Application

The easiest way to insert a graphic in a datasheet is to copy it from another application. This will usually be a program, such as Paintbrush (the drawing program that comes free with Windows), or some other dedicated graphics software, such as CorelDRAW!. The exact steps you use to copy the graphic you need will depend on the software you're using, but the general steps are as follows:

1. Start the graphics application.

2. Open the graphic file you want to copy.

3. Select the image.

4. Pull down the application's Edit menu, and select the Copy command.

5. Exit the application.

When you're back in Access, open the datasheet (if necessary), select the OLE object field in the appropriate record, and then select the **Edit** menu's **Paste** command. Somewhat disappointingly, you don't see the picture in the datasheet. Instead, Access just enters a short description of what kind of graphic you pasted. For example, if you copied the graphic from Paintbrush, Access enters **Paintbrush Picture** in the field. To see the graphic, you'll need to use a form, as described later in this chapter.

Table: Products					
Product ID	**Product Name**	**Unit Price**	**Category ID**	**Discount**	**Picture**
A123-21	Langstrom Wrench	$19.95	4	35.00%	Paintbrush Picture
A456-67	Gangley Pliers	$14.95	4	45.00%	Paintbrush Picture
A789-01	LAMF Valve	$5.95	3	45.00%	Paintbrush Picture
B345-67	Multifaceted Whatsit	$49.95	7	45.00%	Paintbrush Picture
B567-84	Deluxe Thingamajig	$69.95	1	45.00%	Paintbrush Picture
B987-65	7-Sided Whatchamacallit	$29.95	7	45.00%	Paintbrush Picture
C012-34	Enhanced Enhancment Enhancer	$18.95	1	45.00%	Paintbrush Picture
C111-22	Virtual Reality Jockstrap	$9.95	6	40.00%	Paintbrush Picture
C678-90	I Can't Believe It's a Girdle!	$15.95	6	40.00%	Paintbrush Picture
D010-10	The Fruitcake That Won't Die	$13.95	5	45.00%	Paintbrush Picture
D101-01	The He-Man's Cheesecake	$18.95	5	45.00%	Paintbrush Picture

Record: 1 of 52

An Access table which lists descriptions of inserted graphics.

Creating a New Graphic from Access

Instead of using an existing image, you might want to create one from scratch. The best way to do this is from within Access.

If you need to make changes to the image, select the field, pull down the **E**dit menu, select the *x* **O**bject command (where *x* is the type of graphic object in the field; for example, Paintbrush Picture **O**bject), and then select the **Edit** command. The application starts and loads the graphic automatically. Make your changes and then select the File menu's Exit and Return to *table* command (where, again, *table* is the name of the current Access table). If the application asks if you want to update the graphic, select **Yes**.

First select the appropriate OLE object field in the datasheet, and then select the Insert Object command from the Edit menu. In the Insert Object dialog box that appears, use the Object Type list to select the type of object you'll be creating (such as a Paintbrush Picture). When you select **OK**, Access starts the application you selected. Go ahead and create the image you need.

The object types you see listed in the Insert Object dialog box will depend on which applications you have installed on your computer. But, as you can see from the following picture, the types of objects you can work with go beyond graphics to include things, such as spreadsheets and word processor documents.

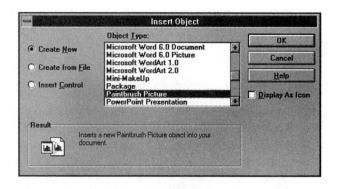

Use the Insert Object dialog box to select the type of object you want to create.

When you're done, you need to return to Access. In most cases, this will involve pulling down the application's File menu and selecting the Exit and Return to *table* command, where *table* is the name of the Access table you're using. You'll probably see a dialog box asking if you want to update the "open embedded object." Give thanks to your favorite deity that you don't need to know what an "open embedded object" is, and then select Yes to continue. Again, Access doesn't show the graphic, but just displays a description.

Using a Form or Report to View Graphics Data

Once you've added some graphics to a table, you'll need to use a form or report to see the images. This is, fortunately, a straightforward affair. When you add an OLE object field to a form or report design (I showed you how to add fields to a form in Chapter 13, "Improving Your Form"), Access creates a large box. When you view the form or report, the graphic appears inside the box, as shown below.

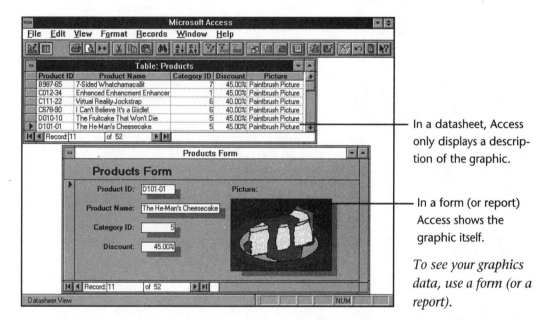

In a datasheet, Access only displays a description of the graphic.

In a form (or report) Access shows the graphic itself.

To see your graphics data, use a form (or a report).

Using Graphics to Jazz Up a Form or Report

Besides using graphics for data, you can also use them to spruce up a form or report. By adding a company logo or other suitable image to your designs, you can add that certain *je ne sais quoi* to your handiwork. There are two kinds of graphics you can add to a form or report:

You'll usually have to move and size the graphic images you add to a form or report. You move images using the same techniques that I outlined for other controls in Chapter 13. Sizing, too, is the same, but you need to be careful: Access normally only changes the size of the box (or *frame*, as Access calls it) that contains the image, *not* the image itself. If you want the graphic to change size along with its box, try this: select the graphic, and then select the **View** menu's **Properties** command. In the window that appears, select **Layout Properties** from the drop-down list at the top, and then select the **Stretch** option in the Size Mode property. Press **Alt+F4** to exit. The image will now change size along with its frame.

☞ Graphic images from another application.

☞ Lines and rectangles.

Working with Graphic Images

You add a graphic image to a form or report the same way you add one to a table field:

☞ For an existing graphic, first start the other application, and then open and copy the image. In Access, open the form or report design window, and select the Edit menu's Paste command.

☞ For a new image, open the form or report design window, and select the Edit menu's Insert Object command to display the Insert Object dialog box. Follow the same steps as described earlier.

Working with Lines and Rectangles

To add some finishing touches to your forms or reports, Access has a couple of tools that let you draw lines and rectangles. Lines are great for separating headers and footers from the rest of the data, and you can use rectangles to group fields or labels together. The figure on the next page shows a form that uses several lines and rectangles.

To draw a line or rectangle in a form or report design window, first click on either the **Line** or **Rectangle** button in the Toolbox. Move the mouse pointer into the design area (the pointer will change to a crosshair), and position the pointer as follows:

☞ For a line, position the pointer where you want the line to start.

☞ For a rectangle, position the pointer where you want the upper-left corner to be.

Now press and hold down the left mouse button, and drag the pointer until the line is the length you want or the rectangle is the size and shape you want. When you release the mouse button, Access draws the line.

The Line button.

The Rectangle button.

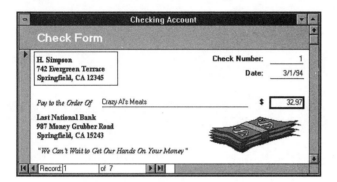

A form that makes use of the Line and Rectangle tools.

Graphing Table Data

One of the problems with tables is they often seem like just a jumble of text and numbers. Sorting and grouping the data can help knock some sense into things, but in the end, you're still dealing with the data in its native format. What you really need is some way of visualizing the data. Well, the good news is that, for certain tables, you *can* visualize your data by *graphing* it.

You can move and size lines and rectangles just like any other control (as explained in Chapter 13). Also, you can use the Palette to change the colors and borders of a line or rectangle (once again, see Chapter 13 for details).

What do I mean by *certain* tables? Nothing special. Access will only graph numeric data, so your table must have at least one numeric field (date fields are okay, as well). For example, the following graph was generated from a table of monthly sales figures for a company. Two fields were used: a numeric field that contained the monthly sales data (which has been grouped by quarter for the graph), and a date field that contained a date for each month.

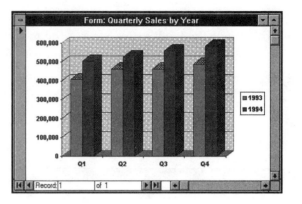

A graph of monthly sales figures grouped by quarter.

Getting Started

The easiest way to graph your data is to use the Graph Wizard to create a graph form. To get started, try either of the following techniques:

☞ Pull down the File menu, select the New command, and then select the Form command.

☞ In the database window, select the **Form** tab, and then select the New button.

To learn how the Wizards work, turn back to Chapter 8, "Using Version 2.0's Handy Table Wizard."

In the New Form dialog box that appears, use the Select a Table/Query drop-down list to choose your table, and then select the Form **Wizards** button. When Access asks which Wizard you want, highlight the Graph item, and select **OK**, or press **Enter**.

Slogging Through the Graph Wizard

The Graph Wizard leads you through one or more dialog boxes that ask for the following information:

☞ The fields you want to include in the graph.

☞ If you included a date field in the graph, the Wizard gives you some date field options. The *category-axis* is the horizontal axis, and you can use the date field for the labels for this axis or for both the labels and the graph legend.

☞ Again, if you included a date field, the Wizard asks how you want to group the data. Select a grouping option from the drop-down list. You can also select a range of dates to use in the graph.

When you're done with the Graph Wizard, Access creates the form and a basic graph. It then starts the Chart Wizard to take you through various graphing options (a *graph* and a *chart* are the same thing).

Choosing Your Graph Options

The Chart Wizard gives you all kinds of weird graphing options. Here's a summary of what happens:

☞ The first thing you need to decide upon is the chart type. The default 3-D Column type will probably do the job in most cases, but if you see another that strikes your fancy, select it.

☞ The next step is to choose a format for the chart type you selected. Again, the format selected by the Wizard will probably be okay.

☞ The Step 3 of 4 dialog box shows you what your chart will look like. It also provides you with six option buttons that can be safely ignored.

☞ Step 4 lets you add some extras to the chart. You can add a legend, a chart title, and titles for the graph axes.

When you're finished, Access returns you to the form and displays the graph. You may see all kinds of extra toolbars cluttering up the screen. You can move these pests out of the way by dragging their title bars, or you can close them by clicking on the small bar in the upper left corner.

Once you've created your graph, you should save it by pulling down the File menu and selecting the **Save Form** command (or by pressing **Ctrl+S**).

The Least You Need to Know

This chapter showed you how to work with graphics in Access. Here's the big picture:

- ☞ Before adding graphics to a table, you have to create an OLE object field.

- ☞ To enter an image from another application, first make a copy of the graphic in the other program, then return to Access, select the field, and select the Edit menu's Paste command.

- ☞ To create a graphic from scratch, select the field, pull down the Edit menu, and select the Insert Object command. When you select the object type you want, Access starts the appropriate application so you can create the graphic.

- ☞ Use lines and rectangles to add an extra touch to your forms and reports.

- ☞ Use the Graph Form Wizard to graph your numeric table data.

Chapter 24

Juggling Multiple Tables

In This Chapter

- ☛ Understanding the table relationship thing
- ☛ Setting up a relationship between tables
- ☛ Creating a multiple-table form
- ☛ Creating a multiple-table query
- ☛ Access juggling skills sure to make you the envy of any circus geek

I learned how to juggle many years ago, and I've kept it up to this day. I'm not very good, but I can't resist a challenge and will, on a dare, attempt to juggle three of just about anything (which, as you can imagine, has scared the heck out of many a party hostess).

Juggling skills come in handy when working with Access, as well. You can create multiple tables and set things up so the information in one table is related to the information in another. From there, you can create forms and queries that combine information from two or more related tables. Does all this require the coordination of a juggler? Not a chance. A little planning and a little common sense are the only tools you need.

Learning About Table Relationships

Many of your Access tables will have nothing whatsoever in common. A table of recipes, for instance, will in no way be related to a table of compact disks. However, tables that *do* have some data in common are not all that unusual.

For example, consider the two tables in this picture. The Orders table holds data for orders placed by customers. It includes information such as the Order ID, the Customer ID (the customer who placed the order), the Product ID (the product they ordered), the Date Sold, and so on. The Customers table contains data about each customer, including the Customer ID, the Company Name, the Address, and so on.

The Customer IDs in the Orders table . . .

. . . are related to the Customer IDs in the Customers table.

Two tables that have a Customer ID field in common.

Notice how the two tables contain a common field: Customer ID. You can use this common field to relate these tables to each other in the following ways:

☞ For any order, you can look up the data on the customer that placed the order. For example, the first order was placed by Customer ID 56789 on March 15, 1994. If you find Customer ID 56789 in the Customers table, you'll see that it refers to Meaghan Manufacturing, located at 887 Green Lantern Lane.

☞ For each customer, you can look up the data on all orders it has placed. For example, Meaghan Manufacturing (Customer ID 56789) placed an order on March 15, 1994 (Order ID 1) and March 21, 1994 (Order ID 9). (There could, of course, be more orders in the table by this customer that we can't see.)

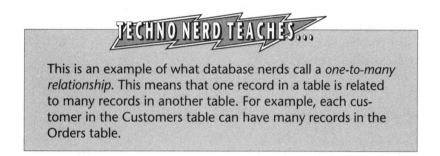

TECHNO NERD TEACHES...

This is an example of what database nerds call a *one-to-many relationship*. This means that one record in a table is related to many records in another table. For example, each customer in the Customers table can have many records in the Orders table.

I know what you're saying: "All this relationship stuff is very interesting, but how does it affect *me*?" Well, related tables allow you to do two useful things:

☞ In a form, you can create a *subform* that shows the data from a second table. For example, if you had a form that showed data from the Customers table, you could have a subform in the table that automatically displayed all the orders placed by that customer.

☞ You can *join* related tables in a query. This would let you, for example, display a dynaset containing data from both the Orders table and the Customers table.

Matchmaking: Establishing Relationships Between Tables

Just because two tables share the same data, it doesn't mean Access automatically assumes they're related to each other. No, you have to stick Access' nose in it, so to speak, and tell it when two tables are related.

If you've been using the Table Wizard to create your tables (as described in Chapter 8), you may already have some relationships set up. (The Table Wizard looks for common field names and asks you if the tables are related to each other.) If you've been creating your tables by hand, then you need to set up the relationships yourself.

Displaying the Relationships Window

To establish a relationship between two or more tables, you need to display the Relationships window. You do this by activating the database window, pulling down the Edit menu, and selecting the Relationships command. If this is the first time you've opened the Relationships window, Access displays the Add Table dialog box. Otherwise, the Relationships window appears as you last left it.

 You can also click on this button in the toolbar to display the Relationships window.

Adding Tables to the Relationships Window

The next step is to use the Add Table dialog box to add the appropriate tables to the Relationships window. (If the Add Table dialog box did not appear, select the Relationship menu's Add Table command.) For each table you need, highlight the table in the Table/Query list, and then select the Add button. When you're done, select Close.

When you're back in the Relationships window, you'll see field lists for each of the tables you added. You'll be using these lists to create the relationships between the tables.

Another way to add tables is to drag them from the database window into the Relationships window.

Creating the Relationship

Unlike human relationships, which may take weeks or months to get off the ground, Access relationships are a breeze to create (the database version of love at first sight, I guess). First, make sure you can see the related fields in each of the field lists. Then, place the mouse pointer over the related field in one table, press and hold down the left mouse button, and drag the pointer over to the other table. (The pointer changes to a small bar as you drag the mouse.) Position the pointer over the other related field, and release the mouse button. In our earlier example, you'd drag the Customer ID field from the Customers table to the Customer ID field of the Orders table (or vice-versa).

Access then displays the Relationships dialog box, as shown below. This dialog box summarizes the relationship you're trying to create. The grid near the top shows the first table and the field you chose, as well as the second table and the related field. If everything looks reasonable, select the Create button to create the relationship.

```
┌─────────────────────────────────────────────────┐
│  ─                 Relationships                 │
│  Table/Query:        Related Table/Query:  ┌──────┐
│  Customers           Employees        ↑    │Create│
│  City            ≑ City                    └──────┘
│                                            ┌──────┐
│                                            │Cancel│
│                                       ↓    └──────┘
│                                            ┌─────────┐
│                                            │Join Type│
│  ☐ Inherited Relationship                  └─────────┘
│  ☐ Enforce Referential Integrity                 │
│  ┌─One To──┐                                      │
│  │ ○ One   │   ☐ Cascade Update Related Fields    │
│  │ ● Many  │   ☐ Cascade Delete Related Records   │
│  └─────────┘                                      │
└─────────────────────────────────────────────────┘
```

The Relationships dialog box summarizes the relationship you're attempting to create.

When you return to the Relationships window, Access draws a line that connects the two fields. This line represents the relationship between the fields.

If you create the wrong relationship by mistake, you can delete it by clicking on the line that connects the two fields, pulling down the Edit menu, and selecting the Delete command (or you can just press the **Delete** key). When Access asks if you want to delete the relationship, select **OK**.

In this Relationships window, a line connects the fields.

Finishing Up

To finish off this task, you need to do two things: save the relationship and exit the Relationships window. To save the relationship, pull down the File menu, and select the Save Layout command (or in version 2.0, you can press **Ctrl+S**). To close the window, select the File menu's Close command (or press **Ctrl+F4**).

Using Multiple Tables in a Form

Perhaps the most common use for relating tables is to create a form that displays the related data from both tables simultaneously. For example, the next form contains data from two tables: the regular form fields display data from the Customers table, and the datasheet contains data from the Orders table. Because these two tables are related by the Customer ID field, the orders shown are just those for the displayed customer; when you move to a different customer, the orders change accordingly.

Customer/Orders

Company Name:	Meaghan Manufacturing
Address:	887 Green Lantern Lane
City:	New Orleans
State:	LA
Zip Code:	90123-0231

Product ID	Date Sold	Quantity	Discount	Purchase Order	Allow Back Orders?
A456-67	3/15/94	500	42.00%	031694-132	☒
D010-10	3/21/94	500	42.00%	032194-089	☒
B987-65	4/1/94	100	40.00%	040194-291	☒
A123-21	4/15/94	750	43.00%	041594-111	☒
C111-22	4/20/94	1000	45.00%	042094-033	☒
B567-84	5/5/94	400	41.00%	050594-155	☒

Record: 1   of 14

Record: 9   of 38

Main form
(Customers
table)

Subform
(Orders table)

*A form showing data
from two related
tables.*

This type of form is actually a combination of two separate forms. The regular form fields (the ones showing the Customers table data, in the example) are part of the *main form*, and the datasheet (the Orders table data) is called the *subform*.

To create a form/subform combination, you use one of the Form Wizards. To get started, try either of the following:

- ☛ Select the New command from the File menu, and then select the Form command.

- ☛ In the database window, select the **Form** tab, and then select the New button.

> **for 2.0**
>
> Be sure to save the main form by selecting the **File** menu's **Save Form** command (or by pressing **Ctrl+S**).

In the New Form dialog box, use the Select a Table/Query drop-down list to select the table you want to use for the main form, and then click on the Form **W**izards button. When Access asks which Wizard you want to use, highlight **Main/Subform**, and select **OK**. The Wizard then takes you through the following tasks (see Chapter 8, "Using Version 2.0's Handy Table Wizard," to learn about the various Wizard dialog box buttons):

☛ Select the table you want to use for the subform.

☛ Select the fields to use for the main form.

☛ Select the fields to use for the subform.

☛ Select a form style.

☛ Enter a title for the form.

When you select Finish, the Wizard first creates the subform and then asks you to save it. Enter a name in the Form Name text box, and then select **OK**. The Wizard then creates the main form and displays it on-screen.

Using Multiple Tables in a Query

The other common use for related tables is to combine them in a query. What's the advantage of this? Well, take a look at the datasheet for the Orders table shown earlier in this chapter. This table contains two fields—Customer ID and Product ID—that are, by themselves, meaningless. For example, without the Customers table displayed, you wouldn't have the faintest idea which customer was represented by, say, Customer ID 22245. (Unless you've memorized all the ID numbers which is, of course, just plain silly.) By the same token, a Product ID of B345-67 could be anything.

The idea behind a multiple-table query is to *join* related tables and display one or more fields from each table in the query's dynaset. So, for example, you could display the Orders table and replace the Customer ID field with the name of the customer and the Product ID field with the name of the product, as shown here. (Just so you know, there's a separate table called Products that contains both the Product ID and Product Name fields.)

Fields from the Orders table

Order ID	Company Name	Product Name	Date Sold	Quantity	Discount	Purchase
1	Meaghan Manufacturing	Gangley Pliers	3/15/94	500	42.00%	031694-132
2	Emily's Sports Palace	Deluxe Thingamajig	3/16/94	250	40.00%	9876543
3	Blowsy's Popside Stand	The Fruitcake That Won't Die	3/16/94	1000	45.00%	C-1293784
4	Emily's Sports Palace	Virtual Reality Jockstrap	3/17/94	2500	50.00%	9876546
5	Stephen's Stereo Shop	Multifaceted Whatsit	3/17/94	100	40.00%	42564
6	Durbin Fire Extinguishers	7-Sided Whatchamacallit	3/18/94	750	43.00%	AB42934
7	Katy's Magic Carpets	Enhanced Enhancement Enhancer	3/18/94	500	42.00%	1234567
8	Phase Contracting	Langstrom Wrench	3/18/94	1000	45.00%	293728193
9	Meaghan Manufacturing	The Fruitcake That Won't Die	3/21/94	500	42.00%	032194-089
10	Switzer Medical Supplies	I Can't Believe It's a Girdle!	3/21/94	1500	47.00%	29381

Fields from the
Customers table

Fields from the
Products table

*A multiple-table
query that shows
fields from the
Orders, Customers,
and Products tables.*

Before you can create a multiple-table query, you need to make sure the tables you'll be using are related. To create the query shown above, I had to set up two relationships:

☞ I had to relate the Orders and Customers tables on the Customer ID field (as described earlier in this chapter).

☞ I also had to relate the Orders and Products tables on the Product ID field. To create a new relationship, first display the Relationships window. Then, select the **Relationships** menu's Add Table command, and add the new table to the window. Now, return to the Relationships window, and create the new relationship.

Once your relationships are defined, you're ready to set up the query. Use either of the following methods to get started:

☞ Select the New command from the File menu, and then select the Query command.

☞ In the database window, select the **Query** tab, and then select the New button.

In either case, when the New Query dialog box appears, select the New Query button. Access then displays the Add Table dialog box. For each table you want to include in the query, highlight it in the Table/Query list, and select Add. When you're done, select the Close button.

The tables you selected appear in the top half of the query design window. Because these tables are related, you'll see lines connecting the appropriate fields. At this point, you simply create the query in the usual way (by adding fields, setting up criteria, and so on; see Chapter 17, "A Beginner's Guide to Queries," for details). This picture shows the query design for the select query shown earlier.

Relationships ⎯⎯⎯⎯⎯⎯

Orders table fields ⎯⎯⎯⎯

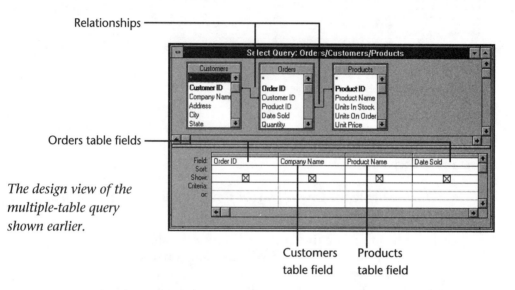

The design view of the multiple-table query shown earlier.

Customers table field   Products table field

The Least You Need to Know

This chapter showed you the ups and downs of juggling multiple tables. Here's a summary of just a few of the tricks you learned:

☛ You can establish relationships between tables that have a common field.

☛ To create a relationship, select the **Edit** menu's **Relationships** command, and then add the tables you want to relate. In the Relationships window, drag the common field from one table to the other to set up the relationship.

☞ Use the **Main/Subform** Wizard to create a multiple-table form.

☞ To create a multiple-table query, add the related tables to the query design, and then add the appropriate fields from each table to the criteria grid.

This page really is blank.

Chapter 25
Access Ideas

Like most people, after shelling out the big bucks for a software package, you're probably determined to get your money's worth. Hey, that's no crime these days. And the best way to get the most out of Access is to stick your fingers into as many database pies as you can think of. To help out, I've suggested a veritable cornucopia of useful—and sometimes even interesting—Access ideas.

Table Ideas

As you learned back in Chapter 8, the Table Wizard has several dozen sample tables to choose from. That's certainly an impressive collection, but it doesn't cover everything. This section presents a few more table ideas the Access designers didn't think of.

Subscriptions

If you subscribe to lots of magazines, a table would be a great way to keep track of things like renewal dates, yearly costs, and so on. Here's a suggested structure for this table:

Field Name	Data Type	Description
Magazine ID	Counter	The primary key
Magazine Name	Text	The name of the magazine or journal
Publisher	Text	The magazine publisher
Phone Number	Text	The Subscription Department phone number
Frequency	Text	Monthly, Quarterly, and so on
Start Date	Date/Time	The date the subscription started
Cost	Currency	The yearly cost of the subscription
Renewal Date	Date/Time	The date of the next renewal
Notes	Memo	General notes about the magazine

You could also add fields for the address (Address, City, State, and Zip Code), if you think you'll need them.

Research

If you collect back issues of magazines that deal with a particular subject that interests you, a table that summarizes the contents of each issue is a valuable research tool. Instead of wading through all those magazines to find the article you need, you could simply perform a quick search in your table or you could set up a query. Here's the structure I use:

Field Name	Data Type	Description
Article ID	Counter	The primary key
Magazine Name	Text	The name of the magazine
Issue Date	Date/Time	The date of the issue
Article Title	Text	The title of the article
Page	Number	The page number of the article

Field Name	Data Type	Description
Keywords	Text	Key words or phrases that describe the general contents of the article. You can use these words for searching or querying.
Abstract	Memo	A description of the article's contents

Software

If, one day, you actually start to enjoy this computer stuff (hey, it could happen), you'll find that software seems to spring out of nowhere. It's a good idea to keep track of it all, and for that you could use the following table:

Field Name	Data Type	Description
Software ID	Counter	The primary key
Software Name	Text	The name of the software package
Developer	Text	The name of the company that develops the software
Version	Text	The version number of the software. (This field is Text because some version numbers include letters.)
Serial Number	Text	The serial number of the software
Date Purchased	Date/Time	The date you purchased the software
Cost	Currency	The amount you paid for the software
Technical Support	Text	The phone number for the software's Technical Support department
Upgrade	Yes/No	Was this an upgrade from a previous package?

BY THE WAY

If you have a home office, you should consider creating a table that tracks not only your software, but all your business-related equipment, as well (computer, printer, fax machine, and so on.). Many insurance companies insist on separate policies for these items, and a table can help make sure you get the right amount of coverage.

Other possible fields for this table include the address of the developer, and the name and address of the store where you purchased the software.

Credit Cards

Credit cards are a permanent fact of life, and they'll remain so for quite some time (at least until debit cards are foisted upon us). One of the basic tenets of good financial management is to take control of your plastic (before it starts controlling *you*). A table that tracks your balance, how much interest you pay, and your credit limit can help accomplish that goal. Here's a suggested layout:

Field Name	Data Type	Description
Transaction ID	Counter	The primary key
Statement Date	Date/Time	The date of your credit card statement
Due Date	Date/Time	The date the payment is due
Balance	Currency	The amount owing on the statement
New Charges	Currency	The total of the new items appearing on your statement
Interest	Currency	The interest charges
Interest Rate	Number	The card's current annual interest rate
Payment	Currency	The amount paid
Limit	Currency	Your current credit limit

You should also consider setting up a separate table to hold general data on all your credit cards. You could use this table to store information, such as the credit card number and the expiration date. You should print this table and store the printout in a safe place so you'll have a reference in case your cards are lost or stolen. Here's a possible layout:

Field Name	Data Type	Description
Credit Card ID	Text	The card number
Name	Text	The name of the credit card company
Expiration	Date/Time	The date the card expires
Annual Fee	Currency	The card's annual fee
Fee Due Date	Date/Time	The date the fee is due
Customer Service	Text	The company's customer service phone number
Lost Cards	Text	The phone number for reporting lost or stolen cards

Stamp Collection

Stamp collectors are a dedicated lot and will no doubt want to maintain a record of their precious collection. This is a particularly good idea for large, valuable collections that need to be insured. Try this layout on for size:

When you create the Interest Rate field, set the Format property to Percent. This will display the rate as a proper percentage. For example, if you enter **.155**, the field will display the number as 15.50%.

Field Name	Data Type	Description
Scott Number	Number	The Scott catalogue number
Description	Text	The stamp's description
Country	Text	The country that issued the stamp
Issue Date	Date/Time	The date the stamp was issued
Quality	Text	The stamp quality (mint, etc.)
Type	Text	The stamp type (hinged, etc.)
Store	Text	The name of the store where you purchased the stamp
Purchase Price	Currency	The original purchase price
Current Value	Currency	The estimated current value
Notes	Memo	Miscellaneous notes about the stamp

Coin Collection

Numismatists can get into the act as well. Here's a suggested layout for recording data on your coin collection:

Field Name	Data Type	Description
Coin ID	Counter	The primary key
Description	Text	The coin's description
Denomination	Currency	The coin's denomination
Country	Text	The country that minted the coin
Quality	Text	The coin's quality
Issue Date	Date/Time	The date the coin was issued
Store	Text	The name of the store where you purchased the coin
Purchase Price	Currency	The original purchase price
Current Value	Currency	The estimated current value
Notes	Memo	Miscellaneous notes about the coin

Purchase Orders

If your company uses purchase orders to order products from your vendors, use the following table layout to record the p.o. information:

Field Name	Data Type	Description
PO Number	Text	The purchase order number (the primary key)
Supplier ID	Text	The ID number of the supplier (assuming you have a separate Suppliers table with a Supplier ID field as the primary key)
PO Date	Date/Time	The date of the purchase order
Terms	Text	The purchase order terms (e.g., Net 90)
Ship Via	Text	The freight instructions
Back Orders	Yes/No	Can vendor back order items not currently in stock?
Cancellation Date	Date/Time	The date after which the order is to be cancelled
Instructions	Memo	Special instructions for this order

Other Table Ideas

Here are a few more tables that might be of use:

☞ Other collections (jewelry, wine, pins, Joey Buttafuoco memorabilia)

☞ Birdwatching (sighting specifics)

☞ Birthdays, anniversaries (who, when, previous presents)

☞ Meetings (how often, how long, how dull, and so on)

☞ Job candidates (qualifications, impressions, and so on)

☞ Trade shows (what, where, when, why)

Query Ideas

Queries are perhaps the most useful of the Access tools. Select queries are a great way to knock a massive table down to size, and action queries can reduce the time you spend on certain tasks from hours down to mere minutes. You'll find endless uses for queries, but this section highlights a few of my favorites.

Calculating a Due Date Field

Update queries (see Chapter 19, "More Members of the Query Family") are great for performing calculations on a number of records. In particular, you can use them to fill in fields that depend on an arithmetic formula. For example, if you track accounts receivable invoices, your table probably includes a field for both the invoice date and the due date. You probably derive the due date by adding a certain number of days (say, 30 or 45) to the invoice date. Instead of doing this by hand, you can easily create an update query to do the job automatically.

The picture below shows an update query that will do just that. Here, the Due Date field has been placed in the Criteria grid, and the following expression has been entered into the Update To cell:

> **[Invoice Date]+30**

This will replace the Due Date field with the Invoice Date value plus 30 days. To make the update go faster, the Criteria cell contains **Is Null**. This tells Access to update only those records where the Due Date field is empty.

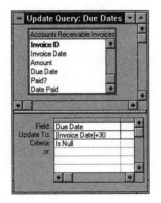

An update query that derives the due date by adding 30 days to the invoice date.

Selecting Overdue Invoices

Once you've calculated your due date for each invoice, the next logical step would be to display those unpaid invoices that are overdue. To do this, you'd simply take today's date and subtract the invoice due date, like so:

Date( )-[Due Date]

Here, **Date( )** is a function that returns today's date and **[Due Date]** is the table's Due Date field from the last section. If the answer is greater than zero, the invoice is overdue.

Since the days overdue calculation will change every day, there isn't any point in creating a new field in the table. Instead, you can create a *calculated field* in the query. You do this by entering the following into a Field cell in the Criteria grid:

Days Overdue: Date( )-[Due Date]

This expression tells Access the following: "Create a new column in the query named **Days Overdue**, and fill it with the formula **Date( )-[Due Date]**." You'll also need to add the other fields you want to see (such as the invoice number, the amount, and so on). This picture shows part of the completed query. Notice how two criteria are used to select the appropriate records: the calculated field (Days Overdue) must be greater than 0 and the Date Paid field must be empty (since we don't care about invoices that have been paid).

A query that calculates the number of days each invoice is overdue.

Making Backup Copies of Your Tables

There are two kinds of computer users: those who have lost precious data through some accident, and those who will. If that sounds pessimistic, well, I guess it is. But it's pessimism born of experience. Accidents—whether deleting a pile of important records or a hard disk crash—can and will happen. Since your data is often irreplaceable, you should safeguard it by making backup copies. That way, when calamity strikes, you'll at least have a safety net to break your fall.

If you don't feel like forking over any cash for a dedicated backup program, you can cook up your own in Access. The first thing you need to do is create a new database on a floppy disk by following these steps:

1. Insert a formatted floppy disk in the appropriate disk drive. I'd suggest using a 3 1/2-inch disk because they have more capacity that the 5 1/4-inch variety, and they are less easily damaged.

2. In Access, pull down the File menu, and select the New Database command (or press **Ctrl+N**).

3. In the File Name text box, type **a:\backup** if the disk is in drive A, or **b:\backup** if the disk is in drive B. When you press **Enter**, Access creates a new database called Backup on the floppy disk.

4. Open the database that contains the tables that need backing up.

Now, for each table you want to back up, start a new query, and add the table to the query window. Select Make Table from the **Query** menu to display the Query Properties dialog box. In the Table Name text box, enter a name for the backup table. Then, select the Another Database option, and enter **a:\backup** (or **b:\backup**, whichever is appropriate) in the File Name text box. Select **OK** to return to the query window. In the table field list, drag the asterisk field into the first Field cell in the Criteria grid. (This tells Access to use the entire table, even if you add or delete fields later on.) Then, just run the query. Access will create a copy of the table and add it to the Backup database on the floppy disk.

The Query Properties dialog box shows:

Query Properties

Make New Table
Table Name: Customers Backup
OK
Cancel
○ Current Database
● Another Database:
File Name: A:\BACKUP

*The Query Properties
dialog box filled out
for a backup copy of
the Customers table.*

Identifying Products Not Purchased by a Customer

Depending on the industry you work in, one of the best ways to increase your sales to a customer is to find out which of your company's products they don't carry. You could then go over this list with the customer to see if you can generate any interest.

Generating this list requires two separate queries. In the first query, use your Orders table to select all the orders placed by the customer. Save this query (I'll use the name **Customer Orders**, as an example) and close it.

For the next query, select the Query Wizards button, and start the **Find Unmatched Query** Wizard. Supply the following information to the Wizard:

- ☞ The table you'll want to see in the query's results is the Products table (or whatever table contains your product information).

- ☞ The query that contains the related records is the one you just created (Customer Orders). To see the list of queries, you'll need to select the **Queries** option in the View box.

This example assumes you have a table of orders and a table of product information that share a common field which uniquely identifies each product (that is, Product ID).

If you have access to sales information for each product, sort the query (or the report) in descending order of sales. This means the first products in the report will be the most popular items that the customer doesn't carry. This information will probably help the buyer make up his or her mind when deciding which products to stock.

☞ For the matching fields, select **Product ID** (or whatever field you use both as a primary key in the Products table and to identify the product ordered in the Orders table).

From here, you specify the fields you want to see and a title, and then click on **Finish**. The Wizard displays a list of all the products not ordered by the customer. You could then use this query (don't forget to save it) as the basis of a report that you could show to the customer.

Archiving Records After Year-End

Chapter 19, "More Members of the Query Family," showed you how to use the Archive Query Wizard to move selected records out of one table and into another. One of the most common uses for this Wizard is to archive records after the end of the year once you're done with them. This keeps your tables cleaner, smaller, and makes them easier to navigate and work with.

To archive the previous year's records, start the Archive Query Wizard, and when the Wizard asks which records you want to archive, do the following:

☞ Select the table's date field.

☞ Select the less than or equal to operator (<=).

☞ Enter the last date of the previous fiscal year (for example, 3/31/94).

Gathering Invoice Data

Chapter 24, "Juggling Multiple Tables," showed you how to create multiple-table queries. If you have relationships set up between an orders table, a customer table, and a product table, you can use all three tables in a query to gather the information necessary to print an invoice (see the next section, "Report Ideas").

Add the three tables to the query, and include the following fields: Company Name, Address, City, State, Zip Code, Quantity, Purchase Order, Product Name, and Unit Price. You'll also need to add some criteria to make sure you select the correct records (the date, the Customer ID, and so on).

Gathering Purchase Order Data

Another use for multiple tables is to gather the data you need for a purchase order. You'll need four tables: vendors (the name and address of the company you're sending the purchase order to), products (the name and part number of the items you're purchasing from the vendor), order details (the amount you're ordering for each product), and purchase orders (the purchase order data, as described earlier in this chapter). Here's a diagram of the relationships you need to set up for the four tables.

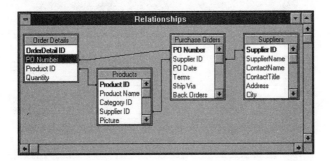

The table relationships for the purchase order query.

Start a new query, create or open all four tables, and then add the following fields: Quantity (from the Order Details table); Product ID, Product Name, and Unit Price (from the Products table); everything from the Purchase Orders table (except Supplier ID); and Supplier Name, Address, City, and State (from the Suppliers Table). To get the appropriate orders, use the PO Number field to enter the purchase order number as your criteria. (See the "Report Ideas" section to see an example of a purchase order report.)

Report Ideas

In Part V, "Impressing Friends and Family with Access Reports," you learned how useful reports can be to spruce up your data and make it look its best. The report design window gives you lots of flexibility when creating new reports, so the only limit is your imagination. This section presents a few ideas that illustrate the power and flexibility of Access' reporting capabilities.

Creating an Invoice

The last section showed you how to create a query that uses three tables to gather the data needed for an invoice. The next picture shows a report design that will create the invoice from this query data.

A report design that will generate an invoice.

Here are a few notes about this design:

☛ The Report Header section contains the data from the Customers table as well as the Invoice ID and Purchase Order number from the Orders table.

☞ The Detail section contains the Quantity field from the Orders table, and the Product Name and Unit Price fields from the Products table.

☞ The fourth text box in the Detail area calculates the extended price for each item by multiplying the Quantity times the Unit Price.

☞ In the Report Footer section, the first text box calculates the invoice Subtotal (the sum of the extended prices). To make things easier later on, I named this text box **Subtotal**. To name a text box, first select it, and choose Properties from the View menu. In the window that appears, select All Properties from the drop-down list at the top and then, in the Name property, enter the name you want to use (for example, **Subtotal**).

☞ The **Tax** is calculated as follows: =[Subtotal]*.05 (assuming 5% tax). I named this text box **Tax**.

☞ The **TOTAL** is calculated by adding the Subtotal calculation and the Tax calculation.

Creating a Purchase Order

The "Query Ideas" section showed you how to create a query that gathered data for a purchase order. The next step, of course, is to place the results in a report that you can send to the supplier. This picture shows a report layout that will create a purchase order.

This report is similar to the Invoice report discussed in the last section. The Report Header is divided into two sections. The top half includes both the vendor information and the ship-to address of your company. The bottom half shows the purchase order data. The Detail section shows the Quantity ordered, the Product ID, the Product Name, the Unit Price, and the extended price (Quantity times Unit Price). The Report Footer shows the subtotal, the tax, and the overall total. I've also included a line for the approval signature.

A report layout for a purchase order.

Sorting and Grouping Ideas

The sorting and grouping feature (see Chapter 21) for reports is useful in all kinds of situations. Here are a few examples:

☛ If you're using reports to generate printouts for bulk mailings, you'll get a cheaper rate from the post office if the pieces are sorted by country and then by zip code.

☛ The grouping feature is especially handy when working with dates. If you maintain daily records, for example, it's often convenient to group the records by month, quarter, or year. No problem. In the Sorting and Grouping dialog box, add the date field in the Field/Expression cell, and then select **Yes** from the Group Header drop-down list. In the Group On list, select Month, Qtr, or Year, as appropriate.

☛ If you plan to keep track of your expenses in a table, it's a good idea to create a Category field and categorize each transaction (for example, Food, Clothing, Mortgage). You could then create a report for this table and group the data by category. By adding totals in the Group Footer, you can track how much you're spending in each area.

Installing Access

Installing software is one of the necessary evils of computerdom. The problem is that most installation programs are written by asocial nerds who figure we'll all know what they mean when they say "Change the BUFFERS setting in your CONFIG.SYS file to 30" or some such nonsense. Fortunately, the Access installation program (it's called "Setup") is better than most. All you do is answer a few simple questions and shuffle the installation disks in and out at the appropriate times (which Setup will tell you). Sound easy? Then let's get to it.

Step 1: Get the Installation Disks Ready

Liberate the installation disks from their plastic wrapper, and look for the one that says "Disk 1" on its label (it should be on top of the pile). Keep the others nearby.

Place Disk 1 in the appropriate drive. If you're not sure which drive is the "appropriate" one, see the following Techno Nerd Teaches. To insert a floppy disk, first hold it so the label is facing up and the letters on the label appear upside down. Then gently insert the disk as far as it will go. 3 1/2-inch disks will snap into place with a satisfying click. 5 1/4-inch disks may require you to close the small latch above the slot.

TECHNO NERD TEACHES...

Floppy disks come in two basic flavors: *5 1/4-inch* and *3 1/2 inch*. The 5 1/4-inch disks are 5 1/4-inches wide (who said this stuff is hard?) and are fairly easy to bend (hence the term "floppy disk"). The 3 1/2-inch disks are—you guessed it—3 1/2-inches wide and come in a relatively rigid case. Before the computer can "read" the information contained on one of these disks, you need to insert it into a disk drive. Look for a drive that has a slot just slightly wider than the disk itself.

BY THE WAY

If you don't know drive A from a hole in the ground, not to worry:

- ☞ If you have only one floppy drive, it's definitely drive A.

- ☞ If you have both a 5 1/4- and 3 1/2-inch drive, the 5 1/4-inch drive is usually drive A.

- ☞ If you're still not sure, assume the disk is in drive A. If you get an error message, press **Enter**, and try again with drive B.

Step 2: Start the Setup Program

Okay, so far, so good. Now to start the setup program. From Windows Program Manager, hold down the **Alt** key, press **F**, and then press **R** (you can release Alt now). Then type either **a:setup** (if Disk 1 is in drive A) or **b:setup** (if Disk 1 is in drive B).

At this point, Setup chugs away for a few seconds and then displays a screen that welcomes you to Setup and contains lots of scary-sounding legal jargon. Press the **Enter** key to move on.

Step 3: Answering Questions

Setup then gets nosy and asks you some questions, as follows:

☞ You're first asked for your name. Type in your name, press **Tab**, type in your company name, and then press **Enter**.

☞ Setup asks you to confirm your name. Press **Enter** to continue.

☞ Setup then shows you your "product identification number." Make a note of this number, and press **Enter**.

☞ You're then asked in which "directory" you want to install Access. Just press **Enter** to accept the default directory.

☞ The next screen asks which type of installation you want to use. The simplest is the Typical installation, and you select that by holding down **Alt** and pressing T. If you're installing Access on a notebook computer, hold down **Alt** and press **L** to choose the Laptop installation.

☞ Now Setup wants to know which "program group" you want to use. Press **Enter** to accept the default ("Microsoft Office").

Step 4: Finishing the Installation

At this point, it's all over but the shouting. The rest of the installation procedure involves nothing more than feeding disks into your computer when prompted by Setup. When you've slogged through that big pile of disks, Access will be fully installed!

It's OK—go ahead and write on this page. You paid for it.

Speak Like a Geek: The Complete Archive

accelerator key   The underlined letter in a menu name or menu command. See also *hot key*.

action query   A *query* that makes changes to a table or creates a new table. Action queries include *update queries*, *delete queries*, and *make table queries*.

active window   The window you're currently slaving away in. You can tell a window is active if it has the blinking *insertion point*, or if its title bar is a darker color than those in the other windows.

alphanumeric keypad   The keyboard area that contains the letters, numbers (the ones across the top row, not the ones on the *numeric keypad*), and other punctuation symbols.

ascending order   A sort order that groups data from 0 to 9 and from A to Z. See also *descending order*.

ASCII text file   A file that uses only the American Standard Code for Information Interchange character set (which is just techno-lingo for the characters you see on your keyboard).

boot   Computer geeks won't tell you to start your computer, they'll tell you to *boot* it. This doesn't mean you should punt your monitor across the room. The term *booting* comes from the phrase "pulling oneself up by one's own bootstraps," which just means that your computer can load everything it needs to operate properly without any help from the likes of you and me.

byte   Computerese for a single character of information. So, for example, the phrase "This phrase is 28 bytes long" is, yes, 28 bytes long (you count the spaces too, but not the quotation marks).

cascade   A cool way of arranging windows so that they overlap each other while still letting you see the top of each window.

cascade menu   A menu that appears when you select certain *pull-down menu* commands.

check box   A square-shaped switch that toggles a *dialog box* option on or off. The option is on when an X appears in the box.

click   To quickly press and release the left mouse button.

command button   A rectangular doohickey (usually found in *dialog boxes*) that, when chosen, runs whatever command is spelled out on its label.

commands   The options you see in a *pull-down menu*. You use these commands to tell Access what you want it to do next.

counter   A field data type that holds numbers that increment (or increase by one) automatically as you add records. These are ideal for creating your own *primary key*.

criteria   A set of conditions you impose on your data. In a *query*, for example, you use criteria to determine which records will be affected. Access works with only those records that meet the criteria.

crosstab query   A *query* that summarizes table data in cross-tabulated form. The unique entries of one field are used as the entries for the left column, and the unique entries from another field are used as headings in the other columns.

currency   Field data type that accepts numbers and formats them as currency values.

database   Any organized collection of information. Access databases usually consist of one or more *tables*, *forms*, *queries*, and *reports*.

datasheet   A tabular grid that displays data in a row and column format. Each column is a *field*, and each row is a *record*.

date/time   A field data type that stores date and time data.

default value   A value that Access enters into a field automatically whenever you create a new record.

delete query   A *query* that deletes records based on the *criteria* you enter.

descending order   A sort order that groups data from Z to A and from 9 to 0. See also *ascending order*.

design view   A window that lets you change the layout of your datasheets, forms, queries, and reports.

dialog boxes   Ubiquitous windows that pop up on the screen to ask you for information, or to seek confirmation of an action you requested (or sometimes, just to say "Hi").

double-click   To quickly press and release the left mouse button *twice* in succession.

drag   To press and *hold down* the left mouse button, and then move the mouse.

drop-down list   A *dialog box* control that initially shows only a single item, but when selected, displays a list of options.

dynaset   The resulting records displayed in a *select query*. Dynasets are "dynamic subsets" of the table data, because changes you make to the dynaset records are automatically incorporated into the underlying table (and vice versa).

edit box   See *text box*.

extension   The three-character ending to a DOS file name. The extension is separated from the main name by a period.

field   A single category of data in a table. In a table object, the fields are the columns.

field name   The name that appears at the top of a datasheet column.

font   A distinctive graphic design that identifies a set of letters, numbers, and other symbols.

form   A data entry window that usually shows only one record at a time. An Access form gives each field its own box and label to make data entry easier.

function keys   The keys located either to the left of the *alphanumeric keypad*, or across the top of the keyboard, or sometimes both. There are usually 10 function keys (although some keyboards have 12), and they're labeled F1, F2, and so on. In Access, you use these keys either by themselves or as part of key combinations.

hot key   The underlined letter in a menu name or menu command. See also *accelerator key*. **Pressing this letter selects the menu or command.**

insertion point   The blinking, vertical bar you see inside *fields* and *edit boxes*; it tells you where the next character you type will appear.

kilobyte   1,024 *bytes* of data. Usually abbreviated as just *K*.

landscape orientation   When the lines on a page run across the long side of the page. See also *portrait orientation*.

make table query   A *query* that creates a new table from an existing one. You can specify which fields to include in the new table, and you can set up *criteria* for the records.

margins   The empty spaces that surround your text on the printed page. Access' standard margins are one inch on the top and bottom edges of the page, and one inch wide on the left and right edges.

maximize   To increase the size of a window to its largest extent. See also *minimize*.

megabyte   1,024 *kilobytes* of data or 1,048,576 *bytes*. The cognoscenti write this as *M* or *MB* and pronounce it *meg*.

memo   A field data type that lets you store large amounts of text.

menu bar   The horizontal bar just below the title bar in the Access screen. The menu bar contains the *pull-down menu* names.

minimize   To reduce the size of a window to its smallest extent, which is actually an icon representing the window. See also *maximize*.

number   Field data type that accepts only numbers.

numeric keypad   A separate keypad for entering numbers found on most keyboards. It actually serves two functions: when the Num Lock key is on, you can use it to enter numbers; if Num Lock is off, the keypad insertion point movement keys are enabled, and you can use them to navigate a datasheet. Some keyboards (called extended keyboards) have a separate insertion point keypad so you can keep Num Lock on all the time.

object   A generic term for any of the items you can store inside a *database*, including *tables*, *forms*, *queries*, and *reports*.

OLE object   Field data type that lets you store things, such as graphics.

option buttons   *Dialog box* options that appear as small circles in groups of two or more. Only one option at a time can be chosen from a group.

page footer   A section of text that appears at the bottom of each page in a report. See also *page header*.

page header   A section of text that appears at the top of each page in a report. See also *page footer*.

point   To move the mouse pointer so it rests on a specific screen location.

portrait orientation   When the lines run across the short side of a page. This is the standard way most pages are oriented. See also *landscape orientation*.

primary key   A unique field that identifies each record in a *table*.

pull-down menus   Hidden menus that you open from Access' *menu bar* to access the programs commands and features.

QBE   Query By Example. A technique that makes it easier for non-nerds to create a *query*. You create an "example" of the records you want to see in the query by selecting *fields* and entering *criteria*.

query   A database object that you use to request information from a table. Most queries display a subset of the table's records (see *select query* and *dynaset*).

record   A single entry in a table. In a table object, the records are the rows.

report   A database object that organizes and formats *table* or *query* data to make it more presentable or meaningful.

report footer   A section of text that appears at the bottom of the last page in a report. See also *report header*.

report header   A section of text that appears at the top of the first page in a report. See also *report footer*.

right-click   Press and release the right mouse button.

scroll bar   A bar that appears at the bottom or on the right of a window whenever the window is too small to display all of its contents. Use the mouse with the scroll bar to see the rest of the window contents.

select query   A *query* that selects a subset (or group) of records from a table. The records selected are determined by the *criteria* entered in the query.

sort   To rearrange the records in a table, query, or report. The new order is given by the values in a selected field. An ascending sort arranges the records from 0 to 9 and from A to Z. A descending sort arranges the data from Z to A and from 9 to 0.

subform   A form that appears inside another form in a multiple-table form.

table   A database object that contains the raw data in a rectangular structure of rows (*records*) and columns (*fields*).

text box   A screen area used to type in text, numbers, or dates.

type size   A measure of the height of a font. Type size is measured in *points*; there are 72 points in an inch.

update query   A *query* that changes the data in one or more fields. The records that get changed are chosen according to the criteria entered in the query.

window   A screen area where Access displays your data.

Wizards   Features that lead you step-by-step through various Access tasks, such as creating tables, forms, queries, and reports.

yes/no   Field data type that accepts only "Yes" or "No."

What a waste it is to lose one's mind.

Index

Symbols

\# (number sign) wild-card character, 140

* (asterisk)
  multiplication operator, 217
  wild-card character, 140
    in query expressions, 179

\+ (addition) operator, 217

\- (subtraction) operator, 217

/ (division) operator, 217

< (less than) operator, 177
  in criteria expressions, 148-149

<= (less than or equal to) operator, 177
  in criteria expressions, 148-149

<> (not equal to) operator, 177
  in criteria expressions, 148-149

= (equal to) operator, 177
  in criteria expressions, 148-149

> (greater than) operator, 177
  in criteria expressions, 148-149

>= (greater than or equal to) operator, 177
  in criteria expressions, 148-149

? (question mark) wild-card character, 140
  in query expressions, 179

... (ellipsis), 37, 42

A

accelerator keys, 34, 275

Access, 13-14
  exiting, 10, 30
  installing, 271-273
  screen
    comparing to desks, 32
    elements, 28-29
  starting, 3-4, 27-28

action queries, 186, 275
  confirmation dialog boxes, hiding/displaying, 225

active window, 154, 275

Add Table dialog box, 246

addition (+) operator, 217

aligning text, form controls, 131

alphanumeric keypad, 26, 275

And operator, 181-182

Apply Filter/Sort command (Records menu), 151

archive queries, 194-195

archiving records, 194-195, 266

arithmetic operators, 217

arrow keys, changing behavior, 226

arrowheads after commands, 37

ascending sort order, 142, 275

ASCII text files, 275

asterisk (*)
  multiplication operator, 217
  wild-card character, 140
    in query expressions, 179

AutoForm button, toolbar, 115

AutoForm Form Wizard, 117

AutoReport button, toolbar, 201

AutoReport Report Wizard, 205

Avg( ) function, 218

axis, category (horizontal), 240

B

backing up tables, 264

Backspace key, 93

Between...And operator, 178

blank records, selecting, 94-95

blinking vertical bar, 91

Bold button, Form Design toolbar, 131

Who cares what you think? WE DO!

We take our customers' opinions very personally. After all, you're the reason we publish these books. If you're not happy, we're doing something wrong.

We'd appreciate it if you would take the time to drop us a note or fax us a fax. A real person—not a computer—reads every letter we get, and makes sure that your comments get relayed to the appropriate people.

Not sure what to say? Here are some details we'd like to know:

- ☞ Who you are (age, occupation, hobbies, etc.)
- ☞ Where you bought the book
- ☞ Why you picked this book instead of a different one
- ☞ What you liked best about the book
- ☞ What could have been done better
- ☞ Your overall opinion of the book
- ☞ What other topics you would purchase a book on

Mail, e-mail, or fax it to:

Faithe Wempen
Product Development Manager
Alpha Books
201 West 103rd Street
Indianapolis, IN 46290

FAX: (317) 581-4669
CIS: 75430,174

Special Offer!

Alpha Books needs people like you to give opinions about new and existing books. Product testers receive free books in exchange for providing their opinions about them. If you would like to be a product tester, please mention it in your letter, and make sure you include your full name, address, and daytime phone.

Also Available!

**The Complete Idiot's Guide
to 1-2-3, New Edition**
ISBN: 1-56761-404-3
Softbound, $14.95 USA

**The Complete Idiot's Guide to
1-2-3 for Windows**
ISBN: 1-56761-400-0
Softbound, $14.95 USA

**The Complete Idiot's Guide
to Ami Pro**
ISBN: 1-56761-453-1
Softbound, $14.95 USA

**The Complete Idiot's Guide to
Buying & Upgrading PCs**
ISBN: 1-56761-274-1
Softbound, $14.95 USA

**The Complete Idiot's Guide to
Computer Terms**
ISBN: 1-56761-266-0
Softbound, $9.95 USA

**The Complete Idiot's Guide
to Excel**
ISBN: 1-56761-318-7
Softbound, $14.95 USA

**The Complete Idiot's Guide
to Internet**
ISBN: 1-56761-414-0
Softbound, $19.95 USA

**The Complete Idiot's Guide
to The Mac**
ISBN: 1-56761-395-0
Softbound, $14.95 USA

**The Complete Idiot's Guide
to VCRs**
ISBN: 1-56761-294-6
Softbound, $9.95 USA

**The Complete Idiot's Guide
to WordPerfect**
ISBN: 1-56761-187-7
Softbound, $14.95 USA

**The Complete Idiot's Guide to
WordPerfect for Windows**
ISBN: 1-56761-282-2
Softbound, $14.95 USA

**The Complete Idiot's Guide
to Word for Windows**
ISBN: 1-56761-355-1
Softbound, $14.95 USA

**The Complete Idiot's Guide
to Works for Windows**
ISBN: 1-56761-451-5
Softbound, $14.95 USA

Other Idiot-Proof Books from Alpha...

The Complete Idiot's Pocket Guides

Cheaper Than Therapy!

The Complete Idiot's Pocket Guide to DOS 6.2
ISBN: 1-56761-417-5
Softbound, $5.99 USA

The Complete Idiot's Pocket Guide to Windows 3.1
ISBN: 1-56761-302-0
Softbound, $5.99 USA

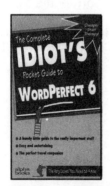

The Complete Idiot's Pocket Guide to WordPerfect 6
ISBN: 1-56761-300-4
Softbound, $5.99 USA

Also Available!

The Complete Idiot's Pocket Guide to Excel
ISBN: 1-56761-370-5
Softbound, $5.99 USA

The Complete Idiot's Pocket Guide to WordPerfect 6 for Windows
ISBN: 1-56761-371-3
Softbound, $5.99 USA

The Complete Idiot's Pocket Guide to Word for Windows 6
ISBN: 1-56761-368-3
Softbound, $5.99 USA